La Tavola

2

La Tavola

New York's
Italian-American
Adventures of the Table

Daniel Bellino Zwicke

4

First Edition
First Edition Broadway Fifth Press 2011, NY NY
Cover Design Daniel Bellino Zwicke

First Published by Broadway Fifth Press 2011
New York, New York   10014

Library of Congress Cataloging-in-Publication Data,
Zwicke Bellino, Daniel
La Tavola: New York's Italian American Adventures
of The Table

ISBN-13: 978-1463618124
ISBN-10: 1463618123
1. Zwicke Bellino, Daniel, Cooks - New York(State)—
New York—Nonfiction, I Title

Dedicated To Lucia Bellino,
Bazzy, Fran Bellino,
Aunt Hellen, Dad,
and The Bellino Brothers;
Frank, Tony, and James
Veterans of World War II

CONTENTS

CONTENTS

ACKNOWLEDGMENTS

I'd like to Thank my Friends, Family, People I have Worked with over the years and everyone who I've ever shared a meal with, at The Table (La Tavola). Thanks to my good friend James Starace who was a major collaborator and host in many memorable Dinner Parties we threw together with girlfriends, Friends, and Family.

Most Thankful Thanks to my Uncle Frank (Frank Bellino), Uncle Tony (Tony Bellino), Anthony Bellino, Debbie Bellino, Sister Barbara, Brother Jimmy, Brother Michael, Eileen Preston, Jason, Lauren, Chad, and Marcus.

Special Thanks to; Joe Macari Jr., Alexandra Macari, Gabriella, Joey, Eddie, and Thomas Macari.

Thanks to friends; Pat Parotta, Gina Parrotta, Maria and Johnny Cataneo, Ronni C., James Bibieri, Jorge Riera, and Raoul Marti.

The FAMILY MEAL

An Italian-American family sits around a table.
The table, laden with Antipasto, fresh bread, salad,
Platters of Pasta, Sausages, and Braciola.

The ritual is classic Italian American at its very
best. These formalities have contributed to making
this country so great.

The United States with its vaste ethnic diversity
and cultural array of immigrants who come from every
corner of the globe. From countries such as Spain,
Columbia, Poland, Russia, France, China, Thailand,
Vietnam, India, Mexico and many more, they all bring
something unique to *The Table of Life*.

We will concentrate on the Italian-Table, Italy,
and its Food and Wine, Italian-Americans, their Food
and the Italian American experience. All members
of the family are busy all week long. There's
work, school, extracurricular activities, "whatever!"

Sunday is the day, if only once a week when the
whole family gets together, brothers and sisters bring
their children to their parent's house. Typically
there are three generations of family gathered
together; Mother and Father, Children,
Grandparents, Grandchildren, cousins, Aunts, and
Uncles. The table teems with an assortment of food,
one course after the other. We start with

Antipasto, moving on to Pasta, then the main course of meat, fish, or chicken, followed by trays of cookies, cake, and Espresso with Anisette.

This is an all-day affair and takes place just about every other Sunday. The family gets together for Pasta and Sunday Sauce (some call it Gravy), the famed Italian-American dish of Sausage, Meatballs, and Braciola. The Sauce simmers on the back of the stove for several hours with tomatoes, garlic, onions, Braciole, Sausages, and Meatballs, before being served up on big platters with either; Rigatoni, Ziti, or Gnocchi.

It truly does not get much better than that! "That's Italian, Italian-American!" I know of no other dish that brings so much Joy and Satisfaction to its participants than this. The dish known to all Italian-Americans as "Sunday Sauce," some simply call it "Gravy." Not only when the participants sit at the table to eat it, but for the person or persons who lovingly prepare the "Gravy," a.k.a. Sunday Sauce. Even before they make it, they will usually get excited, just at the prospect, while making plans, getting the group together and setting the date.

For example, my Mother would tell us kids, "We're going to Aunt Fran's and Uncle Tony's for dinner on Sunday. Maybe it was Aunt Helen's house, or Uncle Jimmy and Aunt Wanda's, but mostly these Sunday Dinners would take place at Uncle Tony and Aunt

Fran's. Aunt Fran and Uncle Tony decide to have the family over for Sunday Dinner. They call my mother, aunts and uncles and invite everyone over. My mother tells me, my sister, and brothers we're going to Uncle Tony's on Sunday. I immediately start thinking of Antipasti, Sausage, Raviolis, Braciola. We might have a Sunday Sauce (Everyone's Favorite), and I'll have visions of Cannoli, Sfogiatelle, and an endless array of Sweets for the four hour long course of Coffee, Dessert, and Chit-Chat.

I'm filled with Joy, I salivate at the thought of woofing down Aunt Helen's Famed Meatballs, and Aunt Fran's Eggplant Parmigiano and Ricotta Cookies. Maybe Uncle Tony will make his famous Veal Marsala. "Life is Sweet."

Happy to be seeing my cousins, Aunts, Uncles, And Family Friends too, maybe Dominik and Sali Banca will stop by, and Charlie Palumbo will Pop over for a bit.

Just the thought of the Food, Friends, and Family makes me Cheerful as can be. So is everyone else. The Scarlotta's, my Uncle Tony's boyhood best friend Jimmy Scarlotta who owns the local "Butcher Shop" will give Uncle Tony the best cuts of meat that he has for our Sunday Sauce. Uncle Tony will pick up Sausages, Braciole, and Beef and Veal for the Meatballs. All the ingredients gathered, Aunt

Fran and Uncle Tony would work their magic and cook the finest Sunday Sauce imaginable.

The whole family will gather round the table, eating, talking, and savoring the food and warm soulful feelings. Sunday Sauce is the Sauce that keeps giving. You always make plenty extra Meatballs, as the Men and Boys must have their Monday afternoon "Meatball Parm Sandwiches."

There is no doubt about it? The fondest memories of my life were the Sunday afternoon meals at my Aunt Fran and Uncle Tony's house on Grove Street in Lodi, New Jersey. Lodi is one of the great Italian-American enclaves of the United States, in fact Lodi is "Soprano" territory, this is where the "Bada-Bing Club" is located. Lodi the town that my mother Lucia Bellino was born and grew up in, along with her parents, my Grandparents Philipo and Josephina, born in Sicily, in the same town that the Sinatra Family and Lucky Luciano came from, Lecara Freddi.

Along with my mother and grandparents were my mother's sister Lilly, and her three brothers Frankie, Jimmy, and Tony who are all Veterans of World War II. Uncle Jimmy and Tony were in the Army in France and Italy, while Uncle Frank was in the Pacific Theater in the "United States Marines."

Grandfather Philipo Bellino had a Shoemaker Shop on Main Street, Lodi next door to the Scarlotta's

Meat Market. Jimmy Scarlatta was my Uncle Tony's best friend and I hear the butcher shop was Uncle Tony's second home. Uncle Tony hungout there day and night. The meat market was his Proverbial Barber shop.

Uncle Jimmy and Aunt Wanda still liveon James Street around the corner from Fran and Tony.I'll never forget the different colored cakes my Aunt Wanda used to make for us, especially the Green and Pink ones. At our house we only ever had yellow or chocolate cakes. Which, naturally was fine with us. We had never seen green, orange, or pink Cakes before. These Colored Cakes mystified my sister Barbara and me. One day when I was about seven years old, Aunt Wanda took my sister Barbara and I into her downstairs kitchen.

Aunt Wanda and Uncle Jimmy had a kitchen upstairs and one in the basement, as did Aunt Lilly and Uncle Frank Pinto who lived on Hunter Street. Aunt Wanda took my sister and me into the kitchen and showed us the small bottles of food coloring she used to give the cakes their different colored hues. We were fascinated. We loved it, as we loved Aunt Wanda and the way she would always have some special little treats just waiting for us whenever we stopped by; Pink Cakes, Green Cakes, or assorted Cookies. We Loved it all!

Sometimes we would have dinner at Aunt Wanda and Uncle Jimmy's house, but it was mostly at Aunt Fran's and Uncle Tony's House that the whole Bellino Family would get together every other Sunday or so for mammoth feasts that would take the whole day to complete, course after "Tasty" course.

These Sunday feasts were one of our families greatest of pleasures. We'd sit around the table with our parents, grandparents, children, and cousins, eating mouth-watering Italian dishes that were lovingly prepared by the ladies of the family, usually Aunt Fran and Aunt Helen. Men contributed too. My Uncle Tony helped cook many a family meal, as I do myself nowadays along with Brother Michael who's quite a Good Cook, as is Cousin Anthony.

To sit around the table with the ones you Love, is quite a wonderful thing. Truly, there are not many things better to do in one's life. I have fond memories of gatherings round the table (La Tavola) eating Pasta with Sausage and Meatballs prepared by Aunt Fran or Helen, listening to all the wonderful family stories our Uncles and Aunts would tell. I'd literally be enraptured and in a state of euphoria, being surround by Loved Ones, eating, and listening to Uncle Frank, Aunt Fran, Uncle Tony, and Aunt Helen. It was wondrous. Some of you may know what I'm talking about, and for those who don't, you must start these traditions of your own. If you don't, you'd be missing out on some the real wonders of life.

Yes, the famous Bellino Family Meals, comprised my mother Lucy Bellino, her sister Lilly and their three brother's; Frank, Tony, and Jimmy, along with all their children which included myself, my sister Barbara, my brothers Michael and Jimmy, and all my cousins. And let us not forget the wonderful neighborhood friends like Charlie Palumbo, Alice Foggi, Dolly Scarlotta, and Dominick and Sali Banca.

It's quite a nice feeling I get whenever I think of those fabulous get-togethers. All those lovely people; my Aunt Fran, Uncle Tony, Uncle Frank and Aunt Helen; all my cousins, brothers Michael and Jimmy, my sister Barbara, mother Lucille, extended family, and friends. My mother's parents passed away by the time I was an infant, so unfortunately I never got to know them and have no memory of them what-so-ever.

I used to love to ring the doorbell of my Aunt Fran's house. Uncle Tony would answer the door and let us in. We'd walk into the kitchen where Aunt Fran would be busy at the stove, stirring the sauce or helping Uncle Tony pull trays of Baked Ziti or Lasagna out of the oven. All my aunts, uncles, and cousins would be sitting around the long

20

kitchen table. They would all say hello as we made the rounds around the table to Kiss and be Kissed by each and every Aunt, Uncle, Cousin, and family friend. It was quite wonderful feeling walking into that kitchen, to see and smell all the fabulous Italian Food, and to have all those dear people who I looked up to and loved so very much, all together in that one special place. The room radiated with warmth. Love. You'd get a similar feeling at a Sinatra Concert, warm, wonderful, Loving, Euphoric.

Aunt Fran's kitchen was quite large. Actually the kitchen is not Large, but as a Child I thought it was. It's the spot where we ate most of those memorable Family Meals. They were quite monumental. These meals would be all day affairs. We usually started them with a very traditional Antipasto of Genoa Salami, Provolone, Sicilian Olives, roast peppers, fennel, and celery sticks. After the cold Antipasto we might have some Fried Cauliflower, perhaps some Stuffed Peppers, or aunt Fran's justly famous Sausage Roll, which was made with pizza dough that was filled with homemade sweet sausage, onions, red and green peppers.

The dough was rolled into a ring and baked. "Yummy!" After these dishes, we'd have either Soup, Pasta Course of either; Baked Ziti, Manicotti, Raviolis, Pasta Fagoli, or Pasta and Peas, which would be followed by a main course of maybe;

Chicken Cactiatore, Roast Loin of Pork,Sunday Sauce, or Uncle Tony's famous Veal Marsala.

We usually would have a tossed salad, Roast Potatoes, Green Beans, or Sautéed Escarole with the main course, and all was good in our World !! The wine that my Aunts and Uncles would drink, was invariably Carlo Rossi "Paisano" or Ernest & Julio Gallo's Hearty Burgundy in either a 3-litre or five-litre jug with the little handle on it. These were real good honest Italian American Wines, wine that were the foundation of the American wine business, dominated by Italians in the formative years of its growth.

This was long before the days of insanely expensive boutique California Cabernets, Merlots, and Meritage Blends.

Our meals up to this point would be about two-and-a-half hours long. Then came dessert and coffee (milk for the children). The array of deserts was always quite astounding. Usually Aunt Helen would bring some cakes and cookies that she baked. On top of that, omebody usually picked up a large tray of assorted cookies, and Italian pastries like Sfogiatelle, Cannoli, Rhum Baba, and Anisette Toast from Sorrento's Bakery on Main Street. For the coffee, Aunt Fran would make fresh brewed American coffee in a percolator as well as pots of Espresso brewedin a "Neapoletan," a special Italian pot for making Espresso.

A "Neapolitan" is made out of two separate vessels that are screwed together, with the ground coffee in the middle. Water is put in the bottom portion, the Neapolitano is put on the stove, the water boils, at which time the pot is turned over (off the heat), and the boiling water flows down through the coffee to produce wonderful aromatic fresh brewed Espresso. A bottle of Anisette was always present to make a delicious Café Coretto. "Ecco!! What more could you ask for?" All those wonderful meals at Aunt Fran's and Aunt Helen's homes linger with me to this day. They always will. This was a dear and wondrous part of my life. The memories are all so very fond, our *Fantabulous* Bellino Family Dinners.

WE TALK ABOUT FOOD!!!

They say one of the telltale signs of a true Gourmand is that as you are eating one special meal, you are already talking about the next one. You only have to pick where, when, and what it's going to be.

It can be at a restaurant, a meal that you cook yourself, or one cooked by a friend or family member. It might be a private dinner party or backyard barbeque. You might be checking out a new place in town. One that has been creating quite a buzz, or you're going back to a beloved old spot, your favorite Bistro, that makes the most amazing Cassoulet a Trattoria for your favorite Pasta, or a Vietnamese Restaurant that makes the Best Pho in town. When the first White Truffles are in season, it's off to the Italian joint that knows just how to serve them, and at a fair price to boot. If a fair price for White Truffles is ever possible. You know, you just wouldn't be a true gourmand if you weren't thinking, talking, and "Dreaming" of that first plate of the season, of the Planets most delectable little morsels, White Truffles, "Ah Heaven."

If you're in Paris you might be heading to Tourd'd Argente for the famously exquisite "Pressed Duck," where there is no place else on God's good Earth that makes one quite like theirs.

Maybe you're going to La Coupole for the stupendous Fruits d' Mere, laden with crisp fresh delicacies of the sea. No place does it like La Coupole with its Grande Café feel of the 1920's, alla "Ernest Hemingway."

If you're in Venice you'll go to Harry's Bar for a Bellini and "Carpaccio" (both of which were invented there). And you might follow the Carpaccio with a plate of Risotto Nero and perfectly cooked Fegato alla Veneziana. In Positano you'll go to Vincenzo's for the Greatest Plate of Spaghetti Vongole on Earth, and, not far away in Napoli you'll feast on the World's Best Pizza Possible. There are actually a few places in New York that can give Naples a run for the money in the Great Pizza department. The Great Pizzeria's of New York being; Patsy's in East Harlem, Totonno's on Neptune Avenue in Coney Island, Lombardi's on Prince Street in Soho, and the Fantabulous Pizza of Mr. Dominic DeMarco at Difarra's in Brooklyn. On top of serving some great pizza, Lombardi's just so happens to be America's first ever Pizzeria. "History!"You'll get the best Sam Tam (Green Papaya Salad) in Assam in North Eastern Thailand, Primo Sushi in Tokyo, and a delicious steamy bowl of Pho in Saigon or somewhere along the Mekong Delta.

There is no place but Philadelphia for a perfect Philly Cheesesteak, Katz's Deli for the World's Best Pastrami Sandwich, and for Fish Taco's it can only be San Diego or Mexico's Baja Peninsula.

"We Talk About Food." When you are in the process of eating one meal and planning for the next, you will get excited by "This Dish" or That; like a great Cassoulet, Bolito Misto, Peking Duck, a Barb- equed Pig, Gumbo in New Orleans, the perfect Fried Chicken (Willie Mae's Scotch House, New Orleans), or Nonna Bellino's Rigatoni with Sunday Sauce, aka (Gravy).

When foodies talk about food, the conversation is sure to include renowned food-products, such as; Prosciutto San Danielle, Fennel Salami from Forloni in Greve, or the ethereal Wild Boar Salami from Dario Cecchini the "Crazy Singing Butcher of Panzano." Go to Modena for the 100 year old Baslamic Vinegar. It is pure nectar.

A true gourmand will fight over which brand of pasta or olive oil is better than another, who makes the best Cassoulet in Toulouse, the best Bouillabaisse In Marseille, the best Cheese Steak in Philly (Tony Luke's), or the best Cheesecake in New York. You will salivate when the conversation turns to rare and expensive delicacies such as Beluga Caviar, White Truffles, or Foe Gras. Why not? After good loving making, there is not a thing on this good Earth that can give one more pleasure or enjoyment than a bowl of Tagiatelle con Tartuffo Bianco or a perfectly made Pate d'Foe Gras. Have a great old Barolo with the Truffles or a fine Sauterne like Chateau Ye'Quem with the Foe Gras and you will be in Seventh Heaven.

One time I was at Caffe Dante and Mario the owner told me about the pasta he made the night before. The pasta is called "Sciaffoni." It is from Napoli as Mario is of the area, Avellino to be exact, which is about one hour east of Napoli and is the home of the famed white wine, Fiano de Avellino.

I never heard of this particular shape before. Mario told me that it is like a large rigatoni. It does not have ridges (rigate) and it is almost three times the size of Rigatoni. You will not find this pasta in super-markets. You have to go to an Italian Specialty Shop in order to get it, and most of them will probably not have it as well, only a very few. You will most likely have to place a special order to obtain a bag or two. Mario talked of Sugo d'Pomodoro for his "Sciaffoni." We started talking about cheese and I told him that I loved to grate Ricotta Salata on some sauces and that you grate it on the large holes of a Box Grater so you get long thin slivers of cheese. Mario said, "No, No Danny, for me, I only put Pecorino on Tomato Sauce!!" Mario was very adamant on this point. Spoken like a true Neapolitan. We both agreed that Ricotta Salata is the proper cheese to put on Pasta alla' Norma. The sauce for Pasta alla Norma is made with eggplant and tomatoes. To hear Mario speak with so much fervor and "Reverence" about his "Sciaffoni" and the fact that you never put any kind of cheese on a Sugo d'Pomodoro, except for "Pecorino Romano," is to hear one truly passionate Gourmand, Mr. Mario Flotta. "Come to think of it, when it comes to being really passionate about food, and Italian Food in particular, what Italian is not?"

Many times when I'm in Caffe Dante on weekday afternoons, I chit-chat with Rose (one of Dante's few remaining Maltese waitress's) about food. It's usually I who starts the conversation about a dish I made the night before, or it can be about a particular way I roast a Rack of Pork, how I make Caponata, my Bolognese, or my justly famous Duck Ragu. Rose will tell me about the way she makes Pheasant or Venison when her husband Tony brings home his bounty from one of his many hunting trips. As we speak, Rose just told me that Tony brought home some Doves the other day. Rose told me she braised them, and said, "Oh My God Danny, they taste so good."Often times I will describe to Rose the way I make this dish or that and she'll start salivating, and says to me, "Danny, please Stop, Stop! You're making me so hungry." That's a fact!

It's great talking about food with friends, or anyone, trading recipes or telling each other where you can get the best Sweet Sausage (Florence Meat Market on Jones Street in Greenwich Village), the most authentic Sopressetta, or the freshest fish. Which butcher is the best (toss-up between Florence Meat Market or Pino's on Sullivan Street), which bakery makes the best Cannoli (Pozzo's or Rocco's), bread, or Biscotti?

Where do you go to get the best prices on cheese and which pasta shop makes the best pasta fresca? Everybody has his or her own favorite places and little secrets.

I remember telling my buddy Jorge Riera (a serious Gourmand if there ever was one) about this great Fried Chicken Salad I had at a street stall in Bangkok. It was phenomenal. In return, he told me the place he thought had the best Pho in Vietnam. I will tell friends about the Spaghetti Vongole at Vincenzo's in Positano, Porchetta Sandwiches in Roma, the Best Burgerin New York, as of this writing, for me, It's a "Toss Up" between The Shake Shack Burger, Peter Luger's, and Minetta Tavern's "Minetta Burger," not the Black Label Burger. In New York who has the Best Burger in town, can be almost as Heated-a-Debate as which Cheesesteak is the Best in Philadelphia, or who makes Chicago's Best Italian Beef. For New York's best Thai Restaurant, go to Shirapaia in Woodside, Queens, and you might start a fight if you want to talk about New York's Best Pizza where you'll find America's Best whether it's Totonno's, Di Farra's, John's on Bleecker Street, or Lombardi's. "Fuggetta-Bout-It Chicago! That's not Pizza, it's Deep Dish Pie, but just don't call it Pizza! Better stick to Italian Beef and Hot Dogs," which you do exceedingly well.

You pass on what you know to one-and-other, the Hottest new restaurant of the moment, a new Bahn Mi Joint, the best butcher for Veal Scallopines and such. You tell each other how to make different dishes and where to get the best products. You are in your own particular network of local gourmands. This is the Passion for Great Food. It is a "Marvelous Culinary Adventure." Explore it. The rewards are great, and oh so very tasty!

We Talk About Food!

"You Talk About Food."

AUNT HELEN

Aunt Helen, my Uncle Franks better half is one of the treasures that have been bestowed upon myself and the entire Bellino family. Aunt Fran is the other. Aunt Helen was born in an area that is one of the most beautiful on Earth. Aunt Helen was born near Salerno, the rest of our family comes from near Rome and Leccara Freddi, a town about an hour's drive south of Palermo. A great deal of the food that the Bellino family eats, are dishes from Sicily and the area in and around Salerno and Napoli, and the food that Aunt Hellen makes is all quite special.

One of my favorite dishes that Aunt Helen makes is her Cavallo Fiore Fritti, breaded fried cauliflower. It is superb, and Aunt Helen is the only one in the family who makes this particular dish, and she really does it well, crunchy and tasty on the outside and soft and subtle Cauliflower flavor within. I love it.

Another one of Aunt Helen's exclusive dishes that we all love is her incredible preparation of "Uovo con Spinaci e Parmigiano." Translated to English, this is Eggs Scrambled with Spinach and Parmigano. Yes, the dish does not sound like much, but these few ingredients when properly cooked are tastier than you could ever imagine, it is truly better than the sum of its parts. If I had never eaten this dish and someone was describing how tasty it is, I'd probably be wondering why this person is carrying on so much over some mere spinach and eggs. I'd be thinking that they might have some kind of esthetical problems. Yet this dish perfectly illustrates the true essence of Italian cooking, getting great fresh ingredients, letting the main ingredient shine, with a little embellishment from a couple others. Of course, the dish has to be prepared properly as Aunt Helen does. I made it once for a few of my friends, Jimmy, Ada, and Johnny. They all went bonkers for it and always request it whenever we have a dinner party.

They all ask me, "Will you please make Aunt Helen's Crostini?" Aunt Helen's crostini is what they call the toasted bread that's topped with the Spinach and Eggs. Aunt Helen used to give it to us as a Pannino (sandwich) on a nice Italian roll. I can still remember the first time she made me one. I had stopped over her house for a little visit and as usual, Aunt Helen always had some food on hand. "Like I didn't know she would. Ha-ha!"

"You want something to eat Daniel," she asked. I never say no to eating some of Aunt Helen's amazing food. She made me this sandwich with spinach and eggs stuffed inside. Aunt Helen put the sandwich in front of me and said, "Here you go darling" When I took the first bite, it was a revelation. I was in heaven! I couldn't believe my eyes (mouth, stomach, and tongue).

That sandwich was "Lip Smacking Good." I asked her how to make it. "You just sauté some spinach in olive oil with a little butter, add the eggs and some Parmesan Cheese," Aunt Helen replied nonchalantly, as if it was nothing. In a way it was nothing, because it is very simple to prepare, simple that is once you know what you're doing. The key word being, knowing, because as simple a dish may be, if you don't know the proper way of making it, you can really screw it up. There is skill, experience, and a knowing touch involved in making it, or any good dish for that matter. You have to season it properly, cook the eggs just so. Not too much, nor too little, and you need the proper balance or ingredients. This dish of Spinach, Eggs, with Parmigiano is what the true essence of Italian Food and cooking is all about.You start with the best and freshest ingredients you can find. You prepare these ingredients in a simple manner, and Ecco, You've got a tasty little dish. That is Italian! That's what Aunt Helen does so well.

Some of the other dishes that we all love, is the way Aunt Helen makes, are; Chicken Cacciatore, her Pasta al Forno, Lasagna, and of course her fabulous

Meatballs.   Aunt Helen's Neapolitan Lasagna with little meatballs is a real home-style dish that you find only in Sicily and around Napoli.

It is the kind of dish that you will hardly ever See in restaurants. If you want to eat this phenomenal dish, you must have a mother, Nonna, or wife who knows how to cook good Italian food. Sadly not everybody is as fortunate as me and my family. We have Aunt Fran, Aunt Helen, and Uncle Tony too. They cook for us, and they cook very well. The kind of food, some can only Dream of.

AUNT FRAN

To me it is without question that my Aunt Fran Bellino has to be along with Aunt Helen one of the finest cooks I have ever known. Well, of Italian and Italian-American Food that is. And what else could anyone ever need? Just kidding, I Love all food, and as much as I love my Italian Classics, I'd be grieving without Chinese, French, Indian, Vietnamese, and all the other foods of the World I love to eat.

But enough about that, back to Aunt Fran and her wonderful way with Italian-American Food. I know quite a lot of good cooks, and believe me, it's hard to beat Aunt Fran's marvelous style of cooking. The entire Bellino family have all been the lucky benefactors of her warmth, generosity and special cooking skills, especially her children, my cousins Tony Louise, and Frankie who were so fortunate as to eat those tasty dishes practically every day of their childhood and adolescent years. Who could be luckier than that?

Aunt Fran has cooked many wonderful dishes for all of us over the years; dishes like Eggplant Parmigiano, Baked Ziti, Stuffed Shells, Manicotti, Pasta and Peas, Escarole and Bean Soup, her famous Sausage Roll, and many more.

Uncle Tony was no slouch either. He actually ran the "Officers Club" at The George V Hotel in Paris during World War II. He was in Paris three days after the Allied Forces Liberated the "City of Light" and the rest of France.

Uncle Tony learned a thing or two over the years, and is a very good cook in his own right. He usually cooks a nice roast meat like a loin of pork, Beef Rump, or leg of Lamb. Uncle Tony also makes a mean Chicken Cacciatore and my favorite of his fine repertoire is his Veal Marsala, which he makes by braising veal shoulder with onions and Mushrooms in Marsala Wine. Fantatstic! I was stunned the first time I ever had it. I had only known Veal Marsala as a dish made with Veal Scallopines (a thin Cut of Veal from a Veal Top-Round or Tenderloin). When I had Uncle Tony's Veal Marsala he cooked for us one Saturday night, it was a revelation. I Loved it, and I now have to say, Uncle Tony's Veal Marsala is the best I've ever had. Thanks Uncle Tony!

Remembering back to the times when my older cousins Connie, JoAnn, Phyllis, Louise, and Tony got married and the family would have great big parties the day before the wedding. Uncle Tony and Aunt Fran would make huge trays of Baked Ziti, Eggplant Parmigiano, and Veal Marsala for everyone to eat. All my aunts and uncles had huge twenty quart coffee urns, the kind you would only see at a catering hall. You don't see many people with large coffee urns in their home, as once it was time for Coffee and Sweets, this part of the gathering was the longest of all. It took three hours at least, and you better have a lot of coffee, especially if a Card Game broke out in the end. They needed those massive coffee urns, all those big parties going on all the time. Come to think of it, they were like caterers themselves, only much better. Their food was and still is by far tastier than any caterer I've ever seen. "I kid you not." They'd make all sorts of wonderful dishes, and Aunt Helen would always make big trays of delicious assorted Italian cakes and cookies.

Of all the splendid dishes Aunt Fran made, there would have to be two dishes in particular that really stood out, though of course they were all wonderful. If I was really pressed to pick just two, I would have to say, they would be her Eggplant Parmigiana and her famous "Sausage Roll." Aunt Fran's Eggplant Parmigiana is out of this World. No one else on Earth can make it as good. It is the "World's Best!" If this was a perfect World, Aunt Fran's Eggplant Parmigiano would be the World's standard of what all Eggplant Parmigiano's should taste like. Aunt Fran's Eggplant Parmigiano is the benchmark that all other Eggplant Parmigiano's should strive to be. Few ever do. It's not easy to replicate. It seems as though when you try Eggplant Parmigiano that other people make, maybe one out of a hundred are good, and that is, if you are lucky. Let me tell you folks, there is a lot of really bad Eggplant Parmigiano out there. It's a sin. It's not an easy dish to make. Eggplant Parmigiano is just one of those dishes that very few people know how to do well, the reason being, eggplant is a bit hard to work with. It soaks up oil like a sponge, and if you don't know how to work it properly, you will end up with a "Mushy Disaster," (which most people do) instead of something ethereal, like the Eggplant Parmigiano made by one Francis Bellino, otherwise known as "Aunt Fran's Eggplant." Needless to say, when making Eggplant most people end up with a disaster.

What they serve in most restaurants as Eggplant Parmigiano, is atrocious. I wonder if restaurants will ever get this dish right? Probably not. I don't see why? I served it, with all its perfection at my former restaurant Bar Cichetti. Well I guess I do know why most places don't make it properly, they were never shown how to make it by the "World's Greatest Eggplant Parmigianino Maker," Fran Bellino. Aunt Fran, she and her "Eggplant" are without a doubt, two of lifes greatest pleasures!!!!

P.S., "I almost forgot. Aunt Fran makes the most Amazing Ricotta Cookies you've ever tasted." One day, I think I ate 10 of them. "Yumm."

ZUPPA!

Growing up in New Jersey, the two thing I probably ate more than anything else were; Cheeseburgers and Campbell's Soups, Cream of Mushroom and Cream of Celery were my two favorites (Andy Warhol "Look Out"). My parents separated when I was very young. On weekends my sister Barbara, brother Jimmy, and I would spend time with our father. Sometimes we would hang around the local area and other times we'd take a ride to the country or down to the Jersey Shore. We used to go to Rye Playland, The Catskill Mountains, Pocono's, and all sorts of places in Pennsylvania, Jersey, and New York.

One of our all-time favorite spots to go to was Palisades Amusement Park, lying atop the Palisades Cliffs, just south of the George Washington Bridge, overlooking the majestic Hudson River and the Isle of Manhattan on the other side of the Hudson. Palisades Amusement Park was a child's dream come true, just a short twenty minutes ride from our house in East Rutherford up Route 46 to the town of Palisades Park where this magical amusement park was located. My sister Barbara and I used to ride the huge Ferris-Wheel, which was in between the funhouse and famed "Salt Water Pool."

It was really scary on the huge Ferris Wheel being up so high, but we felt safe riding it with our dad. The Carousel was a gorgeous piece of working art with its beautifully carved horses, Elephants, Swans, and Sea Creatures. It was simply were marvelous. Palisades Amusement Park was a magical place, where young children could live out their fantasies. We especially loved riding the Beautiful Carousel, as it spun round and round, its monstrous organ churned out a plethora of whimsical tunes, which only added to a young child's euphoric delight.

When I was very young my dad used to put me on one of the smaller horses, he strapped me in and stood next to me, holding me so I wouldn't fall off. My mother was afraid of all the rides. She'd stand on the side and watch us having fun.

My sister Barbara and I really loved the Fun House with the Crazy Mirrors that made you look either; tall, short, thin, or fat. There was also the crazy room with the crooked floors and the spinning tunnel that you tried to walk through without falling. Our favorite ride in the entire park were the Antique Cars that you could drive around on a winding road. My sister always got to drive because she was older than me. I wanted to drive, but I was too small. I could not wait for the day that I could jump into the driver's seat and take the wheel, the same as I dream of sitting in a chair and having my feet touch the ground and the day I'd be able stand at the grown-up counter at Rutt's Hut instead of the children's one. We all used to love the deliciously tasty and salty Saratoga Fries and the cool refreshing Fresh Made Lemonade they sold there. My sister Barbara can still remember to this day where each and every ride was and how the park was laid out.

Boy was that place a ball. Wish it was still there! It would bring back such warm wonderful memories if we could go there again. I miss those days and going to the great Palisades Amusement Park, as I'm sure a multitude of others of the Tri-State area do as well. Along with the Steeplechase and Luna Park in Coney Island, Palisades Amusement Park was one of the area's best and most famous. There was no need for Disneyland back then, in New York, we had our own great parks.

Sorry, got off the track a bit, back to the soup and Hamburgers, delicious, juicy, and slightly greasy Hamburgers. We loved them. Probably close to 90% of the time that we would eat out while on the road, we would eat Hamburgers and Hot Dogs, along with some fries. We would mostly stop at great "Burger Joints" or good old "Stainless-Steel-Diners", whether we were hanging around locally in Bergen County or on one of our many weekend road-trips. We had lots of great places to go to nearby our house in East Rutherford. At that time when we were growing up in the late sixties and seventies, New Jersey was then the "Diner Capitol of the World." Jersey had the most beautiful old "Stainless Steel Diners" around, not like the not-so-interesting modern ones that are out there these days. There was "Tommy's" in Wallington, a favorite of my buddy's and I when we got older. We used to go to Tommy's late at night after a night out on the town or for breakfast on Saturday and Sunday mornings.

The Queen and Peacock Diners were in East Rutherford, Buff's was in Carlstadt, The Tick Tock in Clifton, Rosie's Diner of Bounty paper towel comercial fame was in Little Ferry on Route 46 on the way to Palisades Park, and along with The Colonial Diner in Lyndhurst, The Bendix Diner on Route 17 in Hasbrouck Heights is one of the few remaining of all the famous old Jersey Diners.

Most of the time we would eat Burgers with Fries and a Coke. If we were eating breakfast, naturally we would have Eggs, Pancakes, Waffles, or French Toast. Sometimes I'd have a BLT which I Loved, ever since the first time I had one at the Skyler Diner in North Arlington with my dad. I'll never forget that first BLT with its crunchy bacon, juicy tomato, and fresh lettuce, dressed with creamy Hellman's Mayonaise, in-between two slices of toasted Petcher's white bread. It was sublime!! Every bit as sublime as White Truffles were to me the first time I discovered them, about nineteen years ago. I had never heard of a Bacon Lettuce and Tomato Sandwich before. My dad told me about it that Saturday many years ago.

He explained what it was and I was quite excited waiting in great anticipation for my BLT to arrive. I picked out some songs on the little Jukebox on the countertop of the diner. Dad would always give us some quarters to play music whenever we went to a diner. We loved flipping through the selections and pressing the buttons, B17, L21, E23, etc., to play our favorite songs. Songs from The Supremes, The Monkee's, The Four Seasons (Jersey Boys), Frank Sinatra (Jersey Boy), Tommy James and The Shon-dels, Elvis, and many more. So wonderful, the simple little pleasures of life. Sweeter Simpler Times!

There was and still is not another place quite like "Rutt's Hut." You can find the Worlds tastiest Hot Dogs there. They fry them there, so they burst and crack with juiciness, and you put on their famous mustard relish. They call these tasty Fried Dogs "Rippers" cause the skin rips a bit as they fry. "Yum!" They also have tasty Burgers and Barbecued Beef Sandwiches, but the Fied Hot Dogs (*Rippers*) by far are the Star of Rutt's Huts menu. My brother Jimmy can devour three Rippers in an instant. And he has.

We used to love to order YooHoo just so we could hear the counterman yell out the order in their own special lingo. "One-Mavis-one, One Nude Dog, 2 Burgers two, Traveling." Translation; one YooHoo (Mavis), one hot dog with nothing on it (nude), and two Ham-burger to go. "I loved it." Babe Ruth Loved Rutt's Hut too. He used to chow down there on hotdogs, washed down by a few cold brews so many years ago.

Soup? Mostly Campbell's; Chicken Noodle, Alphabet Soup, Manhattan Clam Chowder, Cream of Tomato, and my favorite Cream of Mushroom. Sometimes my mother would make Minestrone or Pasta e Fagoli but it was mostly canned Campbell's Soup, and at the time in my life I loved them the most, not anymore though. Nowadays my soup has to be homemade, and fresh home-made soup is one of the things I like to cook the most. I often make a Big Pot of Zuppa d' Lentiche con Salsice (Lentil with Sausage) or Italian Wedding Soup of tasty little Meatballs with Chicken, Cannelini, and Escarole. Yumm!

And. Of course, the soups my Aunts made were always a special treat, especially Aunt Fran's Pasta and Peas and Escarole and Bean. Drizzle on a little Olive Oil, spinkle on some Parmigiano Reggiano and you're all set. Just add a nice crusty loaf of Lazzara's Italian Bread and you've got yourself

a complete meal. That's Italian, "Italian-American."
Making soup is great for its economy of cost, it's
a Saver of Time, and it's ease of heating and serving
when you have a batch of Pasta e Fagoli or Minestrone Soup in the frig is a God Send. You make a big
pot, freeze a quart or two, and you are set for a
number of meals to come. All you have to do, is take
it out of the frig, put some in a pot, heat it for a few
minutes, serve, and enjoy. This is why I constantly
extol the virtues of good homemade soup. It's easy
to make, cheap, tasty, and helps you save time.
Once you make a big pot, you're set for numerous
meals, simply by reheating for a few short minutes
and serving it with some nice bakery fresh bread
and butter or olive oil. Soup is great, it's nutritious,
and you can eat it at any time; for breakfast, lunch,
dinner, or anytime in-between.

I was a bit stunned the first time I learned that not
all Americans ate Soup for breakfast. It was when I
was seventeen years old and I was up at the ski house
that my friends and I used to rent up in Chitttenedan,
Vermont, an incredibly beautiful spot. I brought up a
little stash of food stuffs like cookies, Cheese,
Pretzels, and a few cans of Campbell's soup to pop
open and heat up whenever I was hungry.

On Saturday morning, (we usually arrived on
Friday night at the house) I awoke and went down-

stairs to the kitchen where a couple of my friends were sitting at the table.

I pulled out a can of Campbell's Beef Barley Soup, put on the can opener, got the lid off, dumped the soup into a pot, and started heating it up.

My buddy Jay Fahy said, "What the Hell are you doing?" I retort, "What the Hell does it look like I'm doing?" Jay said, "Soup for Breakfast??"

"Why not?" I asked innocently.
"Who the Hell eats Soup for Breakfast?" (Jay).
I really didn't realize that many Americans didn't eat soup for breakfast. We always had, and I assumed everybody else did as well. I don't see why not.

To me if you had to pick only one food item over all others to have for your morning meal, Soup would be my first choice. I don't think there's anything better or more nutritious and easy to heat up, especially when I have some of my delicious Lentil or Split Pea Soup that I made all ready to go within the frig. Soup is great! It's easy to make, inexpesive, tasty, and nutritious. What's wrong with that? And at any old time of the day, breakfast, lunch or dinner and anytime in-between.

"Soup for breakfast???"
"Yeah Jay. It's the Best!!!"

TOMATO SAUCE

After Pizza, Spaghetti Pomodoro (Spaghetti with Tomato Sauce) is the second most popular of all Italian dishes. It is one of Italy's most popular frequently eaten dishes, as well as being hugely popular in the U.S. of A. The dish is eaten by millions of Americans every day, Americans of Italian origins or not, everybody Loves Spaghetti with Tomato Sauce!

When Spaghetti Pomodoro is made properly, it is the epitome of tasty Italian simplicity and economy. A perennial favorite of children, Spaghetti stays with you through adolescence, adulthood, and old age, a good Tomato Sauce is without question one of the World's Great Culinary Treasures, it's inexpensive, nutritious, and Tastyto boot.

Let us clear up a few things about Tomato Sauce and Spaghetti right here and now. There is one massive misconception about tomato sauce that most Americans have when it comes to this great culinary delight. Many people think that tomato sauce is supposed to simmer away on the back burner of the stove for several hours. "No, No, No! Very Wrong!" This falseimpression has undoubtedly come about through people (Non–Italians) confusing the preparation of two different recipes, Tomato Sauce and Sugo al Napoletano.

The confusion probably started by people who were not of Italian heritage. Hearing stories about Sunday Sauce, or various meat sauces such as Sugo al Napoletano, or Ragu alla Bolognese. These and many other meat ragu's that require hours of slow simmering on top of the stove to achieve the proper result of a marriage and maceration of all of the sauces ingredients to blend together. Also, some of these sauces require long simmering over low heat in order for certain cuts of meat to break down and become tender. Cuts such as the neck, shoulder, shanks, and belly.

The primary cause of the confusion can probably be pinpointed to the Sugo al Napoletano in that a large piece of beef bottom round is left whole in one piece and is simmered with tomato, garlic, minced onion, and carrots for three to four hours. The sauce is served without the meat and is tossed with some sort of Pasta, either; Rigatoni, Spaghetti, Gnocchi, or Ziti, while the meat is served as the main course or with another meal. This sauce, Sugo al Napoletana, is flavored by the meat that simmers in it. In essence, this is a tomato sauce that has been flavored by meat, but it does not have any pieces of meat in it as the meat is removed from the sauce and not served with it, but in another course after the sauce is served with pasta and as its own separate course. Got that? The sauce looks like tomato sauce, except it is much darker than a regular Salsa di Pomodoro should ever be. This is how the confusion has come about of people cooking a tomato sauce for hours upon hours. You never cook a tomato sauce this long. Tomato sauce cooks for 45 minutes to an hour 15 at most, depending on the amount of tomatoes in the pot and on the type of pot the sauce is cooked in.

There are a number of variations in a basic Sugo de Pomodoro (Tomato Sauce). For me and to native Italians, the key is retaining the flavor of the tomatoes to their optimum and not overpowering them with other ingredients like oregano, which most Italians do not put in their sauce, while most Americans do. If you really want to put oregano in, it is OK to do so, just don't overdo it.

Most true Sugo de Pomodoro are made with just tomatoes, garlic, olive oil, fresh basil, salt, and a bit of peperoncino (crushed red pepper). All the other ingredients that are put in with tomatoes are meant to flavor it slightly and to enhance the tomatoes own flavors, not to overpower them. Remember you want to taste the tomato.

This is the true essence of a good Tomato Sauce. The olive oil carries the flavor of the garlic, which flavors the sauce a bit, but should not overpower.

The peperoncino is also carried by the olive oil and imparts flavor as well as just a tiny bit of heat. Salt brings out all the flavor of the tomato, and Basil brings its wonderful fresh garden flavors to complete something that is simple, sublime, and in perfect balance. Once you have your properly made Tomato Sauce, you dress the pasta of your choice with it, whether it is Linguine, Ziti, Penne, or the ultimate pasta for this sauce, Spaghetti! Sprinkle on some Pecorino or Parmigiano, open a nice bottle of wine and you are set. A divine meal that is tasty, Nutritious, and economical. It is easy to make and does not require a lot of time to prepare.

When you make your tomato sauce, make enough to get two or more meals from it. You take one hour to make it one day, then the next time you want to enjoy a bowl, it will only take about 10 minutes to cook the pasta and heat the sauce, and you have yourself a nice plate of pasta in a short ten minutes time. "What's better than that?"

Another advantage in knowing how to make tomato sauce is that once you know how to prepare it, then you will have the base for a hundred different sauces, as tomato sauce is what is known as a Mother Sauce. You can make mushroom sauce simply by sautéing mushrooms, adding some tomato sauce, simmer for a few minutes, and voila! You've got a nice Salsa de Funghi! The same goes for a whole slew of other sauces. You can do the same with zucchini, Eggplant, Sausage, Peppers and Onions, Shrimp, Mussels, etc., etc..

You name it! You can make all these dishes and many more once you have this one simple recipe upon which you can build upon. Is that not great or what? You didn't know that did you?

"You've got *Tomato Sauce* The World is Yours!!!"

THE MEATBALL

It wasn't so long ago, about twenty-five years, when the menus in most Italian restaurant in the United States looked pretty much all the same, almost Cookie-Cutter-Like. With few exceptions, most restaurants had pretty much a standardized menu that varied little from one restaurant to the next. They'd have menu items like the standard Cold Antipasto with Salami, Cheese, Olives, Provolone, and Roast Peppers. There'd be Baked Clams, or Clams Casino, Prosciutto and melon, Mozzarella and unripe out of season tomatoes, Manicotti, Lasagna, Ravioli, Spaghetti and Meatballs, the ubiquitous Chicken and Veal Parmigiano, Veal Marsala, and Tortoni and Spumoni for desert. Need I go on? You get the message, and if you're older than forty, you defiantly know what I mean. Then, about twenty years ago or so, some people started opening restaurants that were breaking that old Italian-American Restaurant cookie cutter mold. Restaurants that were throwing out most if not all of the old cliché dishes of the past and replacing them with a multitude of pretty much authentic dishes from all regions of Italy.

Restaurantuers started taking things more seriously, and you started seeing things like Carpaccio, Rapini con Salsice, Parparadelle Coniglio, and Tira mi Su. These dishes that were the new thing twenty-five years ago, but have now become so popular that they too are now cliché as well as the those of the previously old cliché dishes or yore (50's, 60's, 70's). The dishes that were new back in the mid to late 80s are now on the verge of becoming as out of vogue as Stuffed Shells and Veal Parmigiano were way back when, but as they say, History has a way of repeating itself, and those dishes like Veal Parm, Manicotti, and the old lot of dishes are staging a comeback, and a big one at that. Why? Because, they were great , dishes in the first place, they were tasty then (That's why they became so Popular), "they are tasty now," and they always will be tasty. They're just Wonderful Classic Old-School Italian-American dishes, "plain and simple." And because they are so tasty, and such Great Dishes, eventually they stage comebacks. Thus the case with such Popular dishes as Chicken and Veal Parmigiano, Manicotti, and Spaghetti with Meatballs.

There was a point in time when these dishes became so popular that people got sick of them and looked down at them with disdain and bad taste, more or less. Not everyone of course, not Italian-Americans, but a good segment of the general population did. The people wanted something new. With a turn toward the more authentically prepared Italian Food of Italy. The old dishes of American Italian Restaurants lost favor with some people in New York and other parts of the country and the new, more authentic Italian dishes (Italian Regional Food from Italy) were "In" and the old cliché dishes were out. The old cliché dishes started to disappear off menus, but in time the same people who had disdained them for some time, started missing them. They began getting nostalgic for the past and craving nice simple comfort foods, and dishes like Veal Parmigiano, Chicken Parmigiano, and Spaghetti and Meatballs. The old favorites that lost favor for a little while, were missed. In time, these dishes started to reappear. They were revived through nostalgia and simply because they were so tasty and wonderful to begin with, no-matter that they became Cliché, overly popular, and disdained simply for being so popular, no matter that they were tasty as hell. It was never that these dishes were not liked for there flavor, but the fact that because they were so appetizing, people wanted them and ordered them all the time, and for quite a number of years, some people just became tired of them, simply because they were so popular. You could say, they became too popular for their own good, and this was the main reason that they lost favor.

So these dishes lost favor for 15 years or so, but eventually people started missing them, the "Comfort Food" craze hit, and people started craving and asking for these temporarily disdained dishes. These dishes like Chicken Parmigiano, Spaghetti and Meatballs, Veal Parm and others were "In" again. They were coined Comfort Food. People, demanded, and got, once again, Veal Parm, Spaghetti and Meatballs, Manicotti and such.

Places like Rocco's on Thompson Street, Gino's on Lexington Avenue, Lanza's in the East Village, Patsy's on 56th (Frank Sinatra's favorite restaurant), along with a multitude of places down in Little Italy, in "Da Bronx," Brooklyn, and all across America are now busier than ever. Their popularity attributed to the wonderful, comforting old style cooking they serve and the aged décor preserved, as well as the fact that they weren't influenced by the multitude of fleeting trends that came and went. These old restaurants stood the test of time. They stayed old and true, charming, and traditional."Thank God they did!"

In the past few years there has been a craze for So-Called "Comfort Food." Things like pork chops, mashed potatoes, Fried Chicken, and yes, Chicken Parmigiano, as well as Spaghetti with Meatballs, and Eggplant Parmigiano. These tasty old dishes have all come back in a very big way. I'm ecstatic to say how happy I am to see these restaurants so popular again, as they are literally part of our beloved Italian-American Heritage, New York City History, and American Cultural History as a whole.

Although I was utterly happy in the 1980's when there was a great surge of all those new restaurant openings that served authentic Italian food, with a greater array of choices, I must now say that it gives me and a multitude of others, great comfort that we still have a fair number of these old style, so-called "Red Sauce Restaurants" left today. They still stand, and are doing better than ever. We're lucky they were not all totally obliterated. "Dam Lucky!"

Whenever I go out to eat at an Italian Restaurant in New Jersey with my family, I usually order either Chicken or Veal Parmigiano. I never order any of the Specials that they try to get fancy with. Invariably these dishes are not very good. Often someone in our crowd orders one of those dishes and is disappointed. The moral of the story is that when you're in one of those old style restaurants, stick with what they do best, the tried and true, "Old-School Favorites."
Many people will tell you that that Spaghetti and Meatballs or Veal Parmigiano are not Italian. Well Italians do eat Meatballs, but not with pasta. The Meatballs are served on their own with Tomato Sauce or with Polenta and sauce. It was our Italian

immigrant ancestors who first put the two together, Spaghetti and Meatballs that is! Although I must say, that I feel that although it may not have been a known practice, that over time, there must have been quite a good number of Italians in Italy who over the years put Pasta together with Meatballs on the same plate. "It would be absolutely impossible that of the Billions of meals cooked in Italy over the years, that somewhere in homes in Sicily, Campania, Puglia, Calabria, or even Tuscany for that matter, that no Italian mothers or grandmas did not put Meatballs and Pasta on the same plate. "Impossible I tell you! The odds are against it!"

So, what I'm saying is that, although it was not documented, I'm sure that in some households in Italy, over the years, there had to be families who cooked Meatballs in Sauce (Gravy), dressed the pasta, Spaghetti, Rigatoni, Ziti with the Sauce, and threw a couple Meatballs on the same plate as well. Don't you think? Had to be!

Yes, the Italian immigrants at the turn of the 19th Century (1900) were primarily a poor lot. Meat was a bit expensive, and any meal that might include it, would have to be stretched with much cheaper ingredients in order to feed the entire family. That cheaper ingredient was none other than, Yes, you guessed it, "Pasta;" Spaghetti, Ziti, Rigatoni, Cavatelli, and such. I'm sure, some of these Italian ladies who came to America from Campania, Sicily, Calabria, Genoa, and Apulia, as a treat, would put one or two Meatballs on a plate with pasta. Doing this was also a way of being able to wash less dishes.

Did you know that Meatballs are many times more popular in the United States than in Italy? The ratio is not even close. "True," Italians don't eat nearly as many Meatballs as do Italian-Americans, and all Americans for that matter. As everyone loves them. Yes, Meatballs are Italian and they are eaten occasionally, just not normally with Pasta, not that anyone will admit to anyway!

What "Spaghetti and Meatballs" happen to be, is a "Great" Italian American Classic, which is defiantly a cuisine of its own. The Meatballs have been made by scores of Italian-American "Mamma's" and Nonna's over the past 125 years or so. Meatballs, "Polpette," the variations are many and Italian-American boys and men it seems love them much more than the girls do, and they love them best the way Mamma makes them. Some people make them with just Beef, while others make them with a combination of beef, veal, and pork, and in Italy the most popular ones are made with veal. Some Mamma's put in a lot of garlic while others put just a little. The same goes for breadcrumbs. You can useeither Pecorino or Parmigiano, or a combination of both. The two main objectives are that the Meatballs are soft and that they are "Tasty." Make plenty of them and you can make a delicious Meatball Parm Sandwich the next day, another great Italian–American Classic and something that I've never seen in Italy. Meatball Parm Sand–wiches are great never the less.

One dish that has completely disappeared from Italian restaurant menus, are "Stuffed Shells." They are large Seashell Shaped Pasta that are filled with Ricotta and Pecorino and baked with tomato sauce and a little Mozzarella Cheese on top. The ones my mother (Lucia Bellino) used to make were "The Best." They were one of our favorites when we were kids and I used to love when my mom would let me stuff a few of the shells with the ricotta myself. Then when all the shells were stuffed, I'd stick my finger in the Ricotta bowl and lick it, the same way you would do with the bowl of cake batter. "Know what I mean? Yummy!" Now that I think about it, I have not had any Stuffed Shells for quite some time now. Think I'll pick up a box of Ronzoni Shells one of these days and make some stuffed ones for the first time in ages. When I was a child, I didn't know that there were any other companies outside of Ronzoni that produced commercial Pasta. And, although nowadays I always buy Italian Pasta made in Italy, there are two exceptions for me. When it comes to Pastina or Large Shells for stuffing, when making Stuffed Shells, there is only one Pasta Brand and only "Ronzoni" will do."

When I was growing up back in the 60's and 70's, Ronzoni was by far the most popular Brand of Pasta. In fact, as a child, I don't know if I can remember any other. They didn't have all the other imported and domestic ones back in the sixties.

My mother only used Ronzoni, and quite a lot of it, especially, Ziti, #9 Spaghetti, Fusilli, Ditalini, Pastina, and yes, large Shells for stuffing. "Ronzoni Sono Buoni", was their slogan. Meaning, "Ronzoni is so good." I used to use Ronzoni when I first started cooking because I grew up with it, and Ronzoni is a very good product. I stopped using it a number of years ago because when I am making an Italian meal, I use as many Italian products as I can. I use Italian made Pasta, Olive Oil, Porcini Mushrooms, Tomatoes, Anchovies, vinegar, capers, Prosciutto de Parma, and Parmigiano Reggiano.

The only times that I've bought Ronzoni over the past several years is when I get nostalgic for Pastina, and now when I make the stuffed shells in the near future. Pastina is very tiny Star Shaped egg pasta that Italian Mamma's make for their piccolo bambini (little children). When I was a very young boy this was my absolute favorite. I would ask my Mom to make it for me all the time. She used to cook the Pastina and dress them in gobs of butter, and sprinkle Parmesan on top. "YUM yum yum!!!" I used to go crazy for my Pastina. Simple perfection!

"I want some Pastina now, and Stuffed Shells!" For these particular shapes, you'll probably have to buy Ronzoni, for it's hard to find these shapes from other brands.

Think I'll run to the supermarket and get a pack of each. I'll make them in honor of my mother Lucia Bellino. I'll have some Pastina for Breakfast and one night soon I'll make the "Stuffed Shells," and I'll put on some Sinatra, Dino, or Tony Bennett as the Sauce cooks away, "just the way Mommy did."

SUNDAY SAUCE

Of all the fine traditions of the Italian-American enclave in the United State, the Sunday afternoon ritual of making and Eating a Sunday Sauce is Italian-America's most Time-Honored. Mamma, Grandma (Nonna) will make her Celebrated Sunday Sauce. What is it? Well there are a number of variations on the theme. Most Sunday Sauces are made with Italian Sausages, Braciole, and Meatballs. Some people make their versions with; Beef Neck, while others make their Gravy (Sunday Sauce) with just Sausage and Meatballs. Some may throw some Chicken Thighs into this mix. Sunday Sauces can be made with any combination of these aforementioned meats. The meats are slowly simmered for several hours with tomato, and minced onions and garlic. I generally like to make my Sunday Sauce with Sausages, Meatballs, and Pork Ribs. Other times I'll make it with Sausage, Ribs, and Braciole. An old tradition in some families is that mother or Grandma would start the Sauce early on a Sunday morning, get it simmering away for a couple hours on top of the stove, then put it in the oven for a couple hours while everyone goes to Church. When you get back home, the sauce would be ready, ready to be devoured that is.

We would usually start our Sunday meal with the most traditional Italian-American-Antipasto of roast peppers, Salami, Olives, and Provolone. After that, it's on to the Main Event, Maccheroni and Sunday Sauce. Something so Blissfully Pleasurable and Sublime, that it is almost "Sinful."

When a meal centered around a Sunday Sauce is announced, one can have visions of Blissful Ecstasy At thoughts of Eating Pasta laden with Italian Sausages, Savory Meatballs, and Succulent Pork Ribs. All this has been slowly simmered to culinary perfection. Yes just the thoughts can enrapture one into a Delightful Frenzy of the Most Blissful Feelings of smelling, seeing, and consuming Sausages, Meatballs and Gravy. Yes a Sunday Sauce can and does have such effects on one's mind, body, and soul. And, I do not want to sound prejudice, but this is pure fact, it is the Male of the Italian-American species who Love The Sunday Sauce in all its form, far more than the female sex. True! Meatballs too. And Italian-American men and boys Love and hold oh-so-dare, their Meatballs, Sunday Sauce, Sausage & Peppers, and Meatball Parm Sandwiches.

The Sunday Sauce (Gravy) that my mother would make was with Sausages, Meatballs, and Beef Braciole. My memories are vivid watching my mother stuffing the Braciole with garlic, parsley, Pecorino, and Pignoli Nuts, then tying the bundles with butchers

65

cord to hold the Braciole together as they slowly simmered in the Gravy. Another fond memory was helping my mother roll and shape the Meatballs.

As for me, my Sunday Sauce will vary depending on my mood. One thing I Love to do when making my sauce is to add Pork Spareribs to the "Gravy." "Gravy" by the way is what many people in the New York area call Sunday Sauce, particularly in Brooklyn and Jersey (Soprano Territory). Not many people make their Sunday Sauce with the Pork Ribs, but to me they are phenomenal, and anyone who tries them, they are immediately hooked. As I think back, none of the ladies in our family put Pork Spare Ribs into their Gravy. I guess I read or heard about some people doing it, and I believe it was about 14 years ago or so that I started adding the Ribs into my Gravy. I haven't looked back ever since. I Love them, as does everyone whom I serve them to.

Whenever I make my sauce with Pork Ribs, my friends go nuts for them. Many are surprised, as they might never have had Ribs in a Sunday Gravy before. They didn't know that you could use Pork Spareribs. The ribs are traditional with some but not all. It is quite a shame for those who don't add the ribs as they give the sauce a quite wonderful flavor, and the Ribs themselves,. Yumm! The Ribs that simmer long and slow and are very tender," they're so succulent and tender, they literally Melt-in-Your-Mouth.

66

Whenever I make the sauce, and I'm dishing it out to friends and family, I always make sure that I have my fare share of the Ribs. Pork Ribs cooked in this manner, simmering in the sauce are oh so succulent and tasty, they are Beyond-Belief-Tasty. These Sunday Sauce Ribs are, "Out-of-this-World" and friends, one-by-one, go nuts for them.

I remember the time I first met my friend John Cataneo. We were having a dinner party with Ada, Jimmy, Pat and Gina Parrotta, Ronny "C," Bobby Shack. Jimmy had invited John and his wife Maria. I had never met either of them before. John and Maria had eaten already and were not hungry so Johnny told me just to give him a small portion when I was dishing the Gravy out. I guess it was so good, Johnny shyly came back and asked if he could have a couple more ribs.

"No problem Johnny. Enjoy!"
And what to serve with the Sunday Sauce you ask? Any short Maccheroni such as Rigatoni, Ziti, or Gnocchi are best.

The rituals of cooking, serving, and eating Sunday Sauce is a time honored one. It is a quite a beautiful thing, same as making Mole in Mexico or Cassoulet in France. These dishes are all wonderful things of Beauty. They take time and effort to make, and are made and served with Love. These dishes bring together friends and family, and for Italian-

67

Americans, the Sunday Sauce is The King of all dishes.

If you utter the term Sunday Sauce to any number of millions of Italian-Americans, they start salivating at the simple mention of its name. The wheels start turning in their heads, with thoughts of how tasty it is and all the different components; the Meatballs, Sausages, Braciole, maybe Ribs, Beef Neck, or Pig Skin Braciole, the Pasta, and the Gravy itself. They think about sitting at the table with friends and or family, people they love. They'll ponder the Antipasti, wondering what it might be; Mixed Salumi, Baked Clams, Grilled Calamari? And at the meal, there will surely be Wine, Italian Wine, maybe a good Chianti or Montepulciano d'Abruzzo. With Uncle Frank and Uncle Tony, the wine was usually Carlo Rossi Paisano or Gallo Hearty Burgundy, two solid Italian-American winemakers. You think about the warmth in the air, of loved ones, Sinatra, Dino, the Sunday Sauce. "It's a beautiful thing!!!" If you've never done it, "Try it!" If you haven't cooked one for some time, plan a get-together with friends and family, soon. Sunday Sauce, It brings people together, in a most Delightful way, and as the Big Boys would say, "It's a Beautiful Thing."

The MEATBALL PARM

The Meatball Parm Sandwich, as stated earlier, the Meatball Parm is one of thee Italian-American males most treasured things. Things he needs to live a happy, normal, satisfying life. A actual necessities for true Happiness. We ask not for too much!

No you do not have to be a Man or a Boy to eat one. Ladies and Girls eat them as well. It's just that the male of the species happens to Eat 5 Times the amount that Italian-American Women do. Not only that, but the male of the species holds Meatballs and Meatball Parms in much Greater Reverence, than do the females. They "Exalt" it, as the Meatball Parm, it deserves such adulation. The men and boys adore it and get quite excited at the prospect and act of eating one, the "Meatball Parm." And ladies who make them, know how much it is loved, cherished even.

Yes Italian-American ladies and girls love this thing called the Meatball Parm as well, it's just that they don't get quite as excited about this sandwich that is held so dear to Italian men and boys. The Italian-American male have given the Meatball Parm Iconic Status. The Great Ritual of the Meatball Parm Monday and its ties to the Sunday Sauce. You make the Meatballs for the Sauce, The "Gravy." On Saturday you will buy all the meat, the Sausages and the rest of the ingredients for your Sunday Sauce (Gravy) to be made on Sunday. However, on Saturday you are already thinking about those Meatball Parms for Monday's lunch.

Yes Meatball Parms on Monday, following the previous days Sunday Sauce.You see, you have to think ahead. Every good Italian knows that when you go through all the effort and time it will take to make a pot of Sunday Sauce, that you don't just make it for Sunday's consumption alone. No, that would be a waste of time to make just enough to eat on Sunday. It takes time, effort, energy, and work to make a Sunday Sauce, which of course is well worth it. You do not mind the work involved at all, for in the end, the "Rewards are Great," it will yield, the beloved Sausages in Gravy, Braciole, succulent ribs, and Meatballs for Monday's Parms.

It does not really take much more time to make a larger quantity in order to have leftovers for the next day or two, and this is just what one wants to do, is keep that sauce going, and going for another two days is best of all. And in those leftovers are the much Prized Meatballs to use for Monday's Lunch. And it is the men, who Love and need these Monday Meatball Parms so greatly, for the Ritual of the

Monday Meatball Parm is a "Time-Honored" one that must be carried on. Yes, you know this by now.

So, you see, on Saturday when one goes to buy the ingredients to make the Gravy, they automatically know to make sure they get enough ground meat to make plenty of Meatballs that will last the Sunday Supper as well as yielding numerous leftovers for Monday's Meatball Parms.

And if there are leftover Sausages on Tuesday one can make Spaghetti with Sauce and Sausages, or even a Sausage Sandwich. "Think ahead boys and girls!"

And speaking of Sausages and Sandwiches, there is the much loved Sausage & Peppers Sandwiches, and again, more for the guys than the girls.

It is the guys who hold this tasty sandwich in such High Esteem as well. Whether they are making their own at home, having one at a Pizzeria, or at the most popular place of all, The Italian Feast of San Genaro on Mulberry Street every September, St. Anthony's, or Our Lady of Pompeii on Carmine Street in Greenwich Village, New York's real Little Italy. They eat Sausage & Pepper Sandwiches in cities like Boston, Philadelphia, Baltimore, and Brooklyn, and at The Feast of San Genaro in New York, you gotta get your Sausage & Peppers from the "Singing Sausage Man," a Mulberry Street Staple for years.

Yes the Meatball Parm is Dear, it's Loved and Honored. You make the Meatballs, cook them in the Gravy (Sunday Sauce), eat it on Sunday, but make sure there's enough left for Monday, Meatball Parm Day in Italian households all over Italian American America. Get yours.

P.S., you don't have to make a whole Sunday Sauce for Meatballs for your Meatball Parms. Let's not forget the famed Spaghetti and Meatballs. You know what to do? Make extra Meatballs, "You can never have too many."

BOLOGNESE

The famous Italian cookbook author Marcella Hazan wrote in her bestselling book The Essentials of Italian Cooking; "There is no more perfect union in all gastronomy than the marriage of Bolognese Ragu with homemade Tagiatelle." I could not agree with her more, for it is this wonderful ragu that I am most known for. The Journal of Italian Food and Wine wrote that my Bolognese Sauce might possibly be thee best in the country, something I'm very proud of. I take pride in my Bolognese and everything that I cook.

One of my nicknames happens to be "Danny Bolognese," given to me by my good friend Raoul Marti. It is my passion for this wonderful sauce and all meat ragus for that matter which have garnered me the nickname and reputation for making some of the most ethereal Italian Meat Ragus around. I make it "So Dam Good," as I am literally "In Love" with it, My Bolognese. As a famous old actor once said, "No Brag, just fact." It's delicious and the aroma is oh so intoxicating. Besides the enjoyment I get from making and eating it, it gives me a much pleasure to share it with others, my friends, family, or anyone. Feeding my Bolognese to others endears them to me; the same way my aunts Helen and Fran endeared themselves to me and anyone fortunate enough to eat their otherworldly food. The same goes for me and my food, my Bolognese. Why wouldn't it? It's satisfyingly tasty.

Yes, food is a wonderful gift to bestow upon others, and I'm sure you know, it's great to receive as well. The time it takes to cook, for one to specifically cook for others, and grant it as a gift of Love, this is one of the warmest gestures one human can make to another, especially considering you work all week long. Some would not bother cooking. They just want to relax when not at work, and you really couldn't blame them, could you? Of course not. So, you see, when one takes the time and effort required to cook for others, it has Special Meaning. But we do it for love and the enjoyment of it all, Cooking, Giving, Sharing.

Yes I am quite proud of my Bolognese, the way it looks, its incredible aroma that fills the kitchen and creeps through the door to waft through the hallways of the building I live in, in Greenwich Village. It fills the air with its haunting aromas, no doubt captivating my neighbors as they inhale the tantalizing fragrance and say to themselves, "My God somebody's cooking something good. Wish I had some." We've all experienced this, I know I have.

The look, the smell, and above all, its wonderful taste, the Bolognese is beyond compare.

My Bolognese is a perfect balance of Beef, Veal, Wine, Tomatoes, celery, onions, Broth, and a couple of secret ingredients. They simmer for hours until it is has completed the most important part of "The Most Perfect Union in all of Gastronomy," a properly made Bolognese Sauce.

One of life's very sad facts is that few people in this country have ever tasted a truly good, authenticly made Bolognese.

"It's quite mystifying that good Bolognese Sauce is not made more often. It's not a difficult thing to do!"But you do have to know how to do it. It's not hard, but someone who knows how to make a proper Bolognese has to show you. And show you the right way, for as simple it is to make once you have to been shown the proper way, if you are never shown the correct technique, then as simple as it is, you might never be able to do it. Make Sense? It should!

Making the Ragu is one of life's great pleasures. It truly is. It soothes and satisfies your *Mind, Body, and Soul.*

Making and serving Bolognese to friends, family, "Loved-Ones," fulfills that famous old adage in its purest form's, that "It is better to give than to receive." Those givers out there know what I am talking about. You delight as you sit down to share food you've prepared for a deserving soul.

The making of the Bolognese, it is a great experience, an Italian-American ritual, a right-of-passage for some. Put on your favorite Sinatra and Dean Martin records. Take the ride, sipping from the bottle of Chianti, Brunello, stir, listen, whiff the bouquet.

You must first mince some celery, carrots, and onions, then briefly sauté them in butter and olive oil. Then you place your ground veal and beef into the pot with the minced vegetables. You add the wine and let it reduce by half. You will then place the tomatoes, chicken or beef broth into the pot, add a Bay Leaf, a couple Sage Leaves. You are ready to let the Ragu go on its "Long Slow Simmer." The flame is set at its lowest setting. The Ragu should simmer for a minimum of two-and-a-half to three-and-a-half hours.

You can do other things while your Ragu simmers, slowly melding all its fine components of Veal, Beef, Tomatoes, Wine, and minced vegetables, that meld into one of the culinary World's greatest gifts to man, a sublimely ethereal Ragu Bolognese, properly made, is a absolute "Masterpiece," an edible Masterpiece at that. A "Masterpiece" that like the Mona Lisa you can look at, but unlike the Da Vinci masterpiece, this masterpiece, The Bolognese, is edible, you eat it and it produces a ethereal aroma, which you smell as well. And also, unlike the Mona Lisa, you can touch it as well.

I usually start my Bolognese about 3.5 hours before the designated time o f the dinner party. It takes about forty–five minutes to get to the point where all your ingredients are in the pot and you're ready to start the slow steady simmering of the parts. This leaves me time to make an antipasto item that will be ready by the time the first guests start to arrive.

As the ragu methodically simmers on the back of the stove we listen to Frank and Dino; "The Lady's a Tramp," The Summer Wind, Volare, "Luck Be a Lady." We sip wine made by Cousin Joe Macari or perhaps one produced by one of my friends in Italy. We might have Chianti from mi amici Conti Sebastiani Capone of Villa Calcinaia, The Super Tuscan Prunaio made by Alesandro Landini in Greve, or that bottle of 1999 IL Carbonnaione my buddy Jyuri Fiori gave me the last time he was in New York.

Sometimes for the Antipasto, I'll make some Crostini con Melanzane that everyone loves so much. As the ragu simmers, I grill eggplant to top the crostini with. The first time I made this dish for one of our little dinner, everybody went nuts for it, especially Ada, our friend from Napoli. Everybody wanted to know how I made it, for it was so tasty. The Melanzane was gone in a flash.

The Crostino con Melanzane Grilliata takes a good long time to make. I grill the eggplant, stir the Bolognese, drink my Chianti, listen to Frank. "Sinatra that is!" Jimmyboy is in charge of slicing and toasting the bread for the crostini. It's usually at Jimmy's apartment where we have most of the dinner parties we throw. Jimmy along with Ronny C are the DJ's in charge of the music program. I yell at them here-and-there, "Don't play any Crazy Stuff." They usually have a good repertoire, always some Sinatra, a good selection of R & B, some good Classic Rock, Bossa Nova and other Latin tunes, a little Billy Holiday, Satchmo, and a Tony Benett song or two. The music is quite an important element of any good dinner party. Good music helps set the proper mood and is conducive to good eating, conversation, and the enjoyment of each other's company, all conducted in a proper civilized manner. You certainly don't want any awful so-called music like Rap, Techno, or Heavy Metal blaring when you eat that tasty Bolognese. Bad noise like that (I refuse to call it music) just will not do. Maybe it does at McDonalds or Jack in the Box, but not for some lovingly prepared home-style Italian fare. I have gone to dinner parties where there was a nice group of people, a good setting, with excellent food, wine, and cocktails, but the host made the terrible mistake of playing crappy music. His bad choice in music kept the night from being perfect.

A short while after your antipasto is finished; your Bolognese should be ready for eating. You can cook your pasta. You could use tagiatelle which is the most traditional for Ragu Bolognese, but not absolutely necessary. For a party I recommend a short pasta which is both easier to serve and more manageable for your guest to eat. Rigatoni is my favorite and personally, I feel it is better for the ragu than the Tag iatelle, as the sauce gets caught in the holes of the Rigatoni, which is what you want. "Perfecto." Cavatapi, Fusilli, Farfalle, and Ziti are good choices to marry your Bolognese with as well.

After your pasta is cooked, drain it, place it back in the pot you cooked it in, dress the pasta with Bolognese, add a few knobs of butter for richness, then grate fresh Parmigiano Reggiano (Note: do not use Pecorino Romano, it's too sharp for Bolognese Sauce), mix again, and the Pasta is ready to be served. Plate the Pasta and serve it yourself to each guest. Part of the enjoyment when you cook for people, is for you to serve each guest directly. Don't have someone else serve it. You made it and you want to present this gift of Love, personally.

Some nice wines to serve with the Pasta Bolognese are; a good Chianti, Vino Nobile, Brunello, or Sangiovese from Emilia Romangna. All these wines are made from the Sangiovese grape, which goes perfectly with a nice hardy Ragu. Barbera, Valpolicella, Salice Salentino, or a good Montepulciano d'Abruzzo would also be excellent pairings for a Ragu Bolognese as well. Just please, if at all possible, do not serve Merlot or Cabernet Sauvignon with the Bolognese. They would not go well together. These wines are too rich, the Bolognese is rich itself and needs a wine that lighter and a bit more reserved then a Merlot, Cabernet Sauvignon, or Meritage Blend. "If you want the Best Experience Possible," serve one of the Italian Wines I have mentioned above and you'll be in Culinary Heaven. "Believe you me."

So you have a delicious pasta, your Friends, some Delightful Music, and a bottle of tasty Italian Wine. Enjoy!

"Mangia Beve!" This what it's all about!

RIGATONI al FORNO

One of my favorite very home–style dishes to make is Rigatoni al Forno. You will never see this dish on a restaurant menu. "Well almost never." It's the kind of dish that you only get at home, and very few homes at that. Rigatoni al Forno is a dish that is particular to Napoli. It's the kind of dish I used to serve at my restaurant, Home–Style, obscure dishes that are not common in the U.S.. I used to pre-pare it at Bar Cichetti along with "Melanzane Becaficio" Sarde en Saour, and Anatra en Umido as well as a couple other dishes that you don't see that often in America.

These are two things I always strove to do at Bar Cichetti; serve a array of varied wines that most had never heard of, let alone ever drank, and do the same with food as well. I'd find obscure dishes that no one had ever served in a restaurant in the U.S. before.
I'd perfect the recipes, run them as specials, and if people like them, I put them on the menu.

Rigatoni al Forno is the kind of dish that if you're lucky, Mamma or Grandma will know how to make.

Baked Rigatoni is made with; Rigatoni that is baked in a pan with tomato sauce, Pecorino, Mozzarella, and little Meatballs. It is the little Meatballs that really make the dish so special, especially if you are a young child, or a child at heart.You will Love them.

These small Meatballs are very Neapolitan. Sicilians are partial to them as well. One of the most popular dishes in Naples is the Lasagna Carnevale made with these "Little Treasures" of Little Meatballs as well. I love making Rigatoni al Forno for friends. The dish is always a big hit and makes a great centerpiece for any meal. Any friends who've had it will invariably keep asking me, "When are you going to make the Rigatoni with the Little Meatballs again?"I lovethat!" Of course they do! It's the Little Meatballs And don't forget the Sauce!

My ex-grilfriend Dante used to love this dish. I'd typically start the meal with Gamberetti Amalfitana (Shrimp sautéed with Garlic, oil, and green beans), is an excellent pairing to the Pasta al Forno. If you do not want to go through the trouble of making an appetizer that requires a little work, a nice tossed salad will do just fine.

Get a good Taurasi or Lacryma Christi Rosso to go with the Rigatoni. They are both nice beefy wines from Campania to go with the Pasta. "Perfecto!" A tasty Fiano de Avelino or Greco d Tufo from the same region would go perfectly with either the Gamberetti or tossed green salad. Granita de Lemone or lemon ice would finish the meal very nicely, or a fresh succulent Watermelon, if they're in season, you could not beat it. So, try some Rigatoni al Forno. I guarantee, "You will absolutely Love it!"

EGGS!!! ITALIAN STYLE???

You probably wouldn't think of Italians as Big Egg Eaters, would you? Most Americans don't. Pasta and Pizza are what first come to mind as being the most Italian. They are. But if you thought Italians don't eat much in the way of Eggs, you would be wrong. Italians do eat Eggs, and probably more than Americans, except for Italian-Americans who know the pleasures of Frittatas, along with the fiery Uovo en Purgatory and other Italian Egg Dishes.

I'm going to have to let you in on a little secret. Italians love that cute little white marvel of nature quite a lot. Americans may consume a greater number of eggs per capita, but they wouldn't be able to touch the Italians for tastiness and variety of preparations.

Most Americans eat eggs for breakfast, that's it. They usually have them boiled, scrambled, poached, or fried without any other seasonings other than salt and pepper, and or what the French like to call Sauce American (Ketchup). The way most people eat their eggs in the states is quite boring and bland. They get the flavor on the plate from the likes of bacon, sausage, ham, and home-fried potatoes, unless they are eating some kind of an omelet or Eggs Benedict. Italians on the other hand prepare a tasty array of all sorts of Egg recipes. Recipes that are exceedingly more interesting and diverse than what you see on the American plate.

It should be pointed out that theItalians usually have their eggs for lunch or dinner rather than breakfast.

In Italy they make wonderful flat omelets called Frittata that can be made with an endless array of ingredients, such as; Asparagus, Potato and Onion, Zucchini and Peppers, Wild Mushrooms, Sausage and Pepper, or Spaghetti with tomato and Parmigiano. The list goes on-and-on.

The frittata can be made thick or thin. When they are made thin you can make Pannini with them as well. When made thick, you can cut them into wedges to serve as part of a mixed antipasto, put in your lunchbox, or take along on a picnic, and they're wonderful to bring along to snack on whenever you are taking a long trip in the car.

Frittata are a great vehicle for using up leftovers, something the Italians excel at. If you have any vegetables leftover from a meal, you can sauté them in a non-stick pan that you will make the frittata in. You beat a few eggs with salt and pepper, add them to the pan, cook until the eggs set, adding some grated cheese, and voila! Presto! You've made a Frittata and you're ready to cut it into wedges; eat on the spot, or pack into your Lunch–Bucket or Picnic Basket, they are absolutely perfect.

If you have any type of leftover meat, poultry, or fish, you chop it into small pieces, sauté it with a little butter or olive oil, adding whatever other ingredient you'd like to add flavor with, such as garlic, onions, Parmigiano, and or fresh herbs, whatever you want. Add the eggs, cook and you have just made another frittata. "Simple as that!"

You can serve the Frittata with a salad and some bread, and you are set with a nice little meal in a matter of minutes. And any leftover, you can leave in the frig, and cut off a wedge whenever you hunger for a nice little snack.

Frittata are incredibly easy and fast to make. Once you know the basic method of cooking them, you will have added to your repertoire, at least another hundred dishes simply by changing the ingredients to whatever you want to make yours out of.

Some of my personal favorites are with Sausage & Peppers, with Broccoli and Goat Cheese, or Potato and Pancetta. Once you learn how to make them, you get addicted to making many different types, and trying out your own special creations. Italians also serve eggs baked over a bed of sautéed spinach, sprinkled with Parmigiano, Uovo en Purgotory (eggs poached in spicy tomato sauce), or the most luxurious and decadent Egg Dish of all Scramble Eggs with White Truffles shaved on top.

One of my all-time favorite Italian egg dishes is Asparigi Milanese. For this dish you bake asparagus with butter and Parmigiano, and top with a fried egg. "Yummm." It is funny to see how amazed people are when I cook one of the various Italian Egg preparations of which they have never seen before. They are particularly surprised at the use of ingredients and how tasty these dishes are. They can't believe it. "Ah, the wonders of the Italian Egg Repertoire." You never would have guessed it!

Lunch with FRANK ? *"Sinatra That Is!"*

It was one fine day about fourteen years ago that I was going to a have lunch at Trattoria Spaghetto on Carmine Street with my good friend James Starace. Jimmy was living in Staten Island at the time and I was in the same place in Greenwich Village where I still reside today. We rendezvoused on Broadway and started making our way towards the Trattoria when all of a sudden, I had a change of heart. I didn't feel like going to a restaurant. Instead, I had the urge to have some good old home cooked food. A thought came into my head. I had made a nice pot of Bolognese Sauce a couple nights before and was really in the mood for that as opposed to eating at the Trattoria. Although the pasta there is very good, it's not quite as good as mine, "There's no doubt about that!" I asked Jimmy if he wanted to have some Rigatoni Bolognese over at my place. Jimmy declined, "No thanks. It's such a beautiful day. I want to eat outside," he said. I retorted, "OK." We continued west on Bleecker Street for another block when another idea came to me. So I asked Jimmyboy, "How bout if I make the pasta and we eat it outside at the playground next to my place?" The same playground, by-the-way that Eric Roberts, Tony Musante (Greenwich Village Native), and Mickey

Rourke played stickball in to the sounds of Frank Sinatra's "Summer Wind" in the movie, "The Pope of Greenwich Village." A great movie about a couple of Italian— American cousins in the West Village that gave people a nice little insight into the lives of a of young Italian guys from the neighborhood. Eric Roberts and Mickey Rourke both turned in wonderful performances, as well as Burt Young as "Bed Bug Eddie" and a fabulous piece of acting by Geraldine Paige as the mother of "Buncky" a slightly Crooked Cop who was on the take from "The Bed Bug."

Anyway, Jimmy said yes to the idea. So we went to my place, I cooked the pasta, grabbed a bottle of Chianti, bread, and some water, along with my Sinatra Live at the Sands" CD and my portable CD player. We took everything out to the Houston Street Playground and parked ourselves on a bench at the southern end of the park. I popped in the Sinatra CD and we began to eat our pasta. We drank our Chianti and listened to Frank.

The lunch was superb. Why wouldn't it be? We were eating my Bolognese to the sounds of Sinatra, drinking Chianti in Greenwich Village, New York, outs ide on a beautiful Spring Day. It was a beautiful day in The Village. My bud Jimmy and I had one of those Serendipitously unplanned times that always stays in your memory. To this day, almost 15 years

91

later, I still think of the lunch that day. Lunch with Frank, Jimmy, and The Bolognese.

Well, yes we did plan to get together and have lunch but not in that manner, outside at a play-ground in New York's Greenwich Village. It turned out beautifully, and if we ate at the Trattoria that day, I doubt if we'd still be talking about it till this very day.

Another notable thing about the day was that it was the starting point of a great and wonderful ritual of ours. As a result of our day of sharing "The Bolognese"that day in the playground, Jimmy and I got the idea to start throwing Italian Dinner Parties. The gathering of friends that became "La Bella Tavola" thanks to my cooking, Jimmy, Frank (Sinatra), and the ideal day on Houston Street, and a impromptu lunch, Lunch with "Frank," Frank Sinatra.

LA BELLA TAVOLA

La Tavola de Amici, "The Table of Friends" is made up of; myself, my pal Jimmy Starace and his fiancé Tanya, Ada from Napoli, Ronni C, Pat and Gina Parrotta, Patricia, John and Maria Cataneo, Professor Loyd, Jorge Riera, Bobby Shack, Rose and her husband Tony and a few other assorted characters. Not all of these characters are always present except for me, my buddy Jimmy, and his fiancé Tanya. I'm the cook and the parties are usually at Jimmy's place. We are the hosts. We have our usual core group of friends and a few other outsiders that we now and then invite in.

These dinners are primarily Italian meals, about 95% of the time, although I might make Paella, Fish Tacos, Bouillabaisse or a nice Thai dinner on occasion. The meals are Italian, as are we. We grew up with this food, and it's the food I cook best.

So, most of the time, it's Italian.Usually our dinners are based around Pasta (not always) as the main course, and for good reason. Number one being we are Italian and we "Love Our Pasta" most of all. Number two, is that the apartment is small, with very little prep space. We always have a great time and one of the ideas is not to have to do a ton of work, though quite often the work involved is substantial. We do try to keep the amount of work to a minimum. It's usually easiest for me to cook a Pasta that everyone likes. We always start with some sort of Antipasto. The antipasto can be as simple as a mixed green salad or the traditional Italian-American favorite of mixed cured meats like Salami, Prosciutto, and Mortadella, with some Provolone, and Olives. These items are delicious and don't require any work to serve, other than going to the Italian market to pick them up, and laying them out on a plate. Putting out an Antipasto like that gives me some more time to relax and socialize. However, this being said, often I'll make one of any number of Antipasti dishes from my repertoire. It's more work but I don't mind. My guest seem to like it better and are often times requesting I make one of my most popular dishes dishes, like; "Caponata,"some sort of Frittata, Melazane alla Griglia, Crostini con Funghi, Stuffed Mushrooms, or Crostino Helena. My friends often request the Caponata or Crostino Helena especially Ada), which is one of a number of tasty dishes Aunt Helen taught me how to make.

Not many people know about this dish. It is not in any cookbooks. It is one of Aunt Helen's family recipes from Salerno. It consists of Spinach that is chopped and sautéed in butter and olive oil with minced onions. Beaten eggs are added, as well as

Parmigiano, salt, and pepper. This dish is not actually a frittata, but Italian Scrambled Eggs (Uovo Strapizatte) that are cooked in butter and olive oil with Spinach and Parmigiano. "The dish is absolutely delicious!" You serve it on top of a piece of toasted bread as a crostini or as a sandwich as we usually do for a nice lite lunch over at Aunt Helen's house.

Another tasty item to serve for Antipasto is Caponata. Caponata is a wonderful Sicilian specialty. Pasta con Sarde is the most famous savory dish from Sicily, but to me "Caponata" is the best one, along with Cannoli which without a doubt, is Sicily's most famous food item of all. My mother "Lucia" weaned us on these lovely little morsels of fried anise flavored dough shells that are stuffed with sweetened Ricotta Cheese and sprinkled with chopped toasted Pistachio Nuts. Of course there are many superb dishes in the Sicilian repertoire. Most Americans know very little of Sicilian food, but our family being from Sicily, we know it quite well. One of my favorites is Vinny's ethereal Vasteddi Sandwiches. Vastedda is a Fam-ous Sandwich of Palermo that is made with fried Beef Spleen, Cacciocavallo Cheese, and Ricotta. Those less adventurous than me would *say, "Yuck" to Beef Spleen, but this sandwich is rather scrumptious. I discovered it not in Palermo* but at my friend Vinny's place "La Foccaceria" on First Avenue in

The East Village. La Foccaceria is a great little Trattoria that makes other wonderful Sicilian specialties like Arancini (Rice Balls) and Sfincione. La Foccaceria is the only place in all of Manhattan where you can get one of these wonderful Vasttedi Sandwiches. They are truly amazing, and at only $2.50 a Pop, one of New York's great food bargains. Vinny, is also one of the few people in New York to make Sfingione, the tasty Sicilian Pizza made with a topping of onions that are slowly sautéed with Anchovies until sublimely Sweet and Savory, and mixed with Breadcrumbs and a bit of Garlic. This Pizza is outstanding, and Vinny makes it on Thursdays and Saturdays, the day all the Old Guys who moved out of the Old Neighborhood and off to Brooklyn, Staten Island, or Long Island, make their way to the East Village and La Focceria to meet-up and eat "Vinny's otherworldly Vasttedi Sandwiches," Sfingione, and nourishing Lentil and Escarole Soup too. La Foccaceria has been around for more than 60 years, a real East Village Sicilian-American institution. Vinny's father started the place way back when on First Avenue between 11th and 12th Streets.

I never went to to La Foccaceria when it was a few blocks north of the current location on, still First Avenue, but now between 7th Street and St. Mark's

Place. I started going there in the Summer of 1985, right after getting back from my first trip to Italy.

Ah, if only I could go back in time. Of all my wonderful trips to Italy, this one was the Sweetest and most exciting, discovering Italy, its Food, Art, Churches, Fountains, Piazzas, Wine, and people for the first time. One of the most wonderful things in my life. That trip was so special as I still had that childlike feelings for the place. Feelings that make things so much more special, Magical. Kind of like a Child on Christmas Day feelings, if you know what I mean.

Anyway, back to Vinny's, the place is one of a kind, "You just Gotta Try it," especially the Vasttedda. "Come on now, don't be a Whimp."

OK, let's get back to the "Caponata." What is it you ask? It's a sweet and sour vegetable stew that's made up of primarily of Eggplant that is cooked with Onions, Tomato, Celery, Raisons, Sugar, Vinegar, Capers, and some other exotic things that I put in mine but I can't tell you, or "I'd have to Kill You." Each cook has their own special recipe, just like other great dishes of the World; like Cassoulet, Gumbo, Bouillabaisse, and many, many more.

Each individual gives it their own distinctive uniqueness that only they can do. This is one of the many joys of good eating and cooking, the endless array of food, restaurants, and the deciding factor that varied techniques from different cooks providing for a fabulous never ending journey of the foods of the World. Caponata is very versatile and can be eaten on its own, or as part of an Antipasto Platter, on a Pannino, or as an accompaniment to a main course of fish, poultry, or meat.

As for the Pasta at our parties, some of the favorites that I make are; Parparadelle con Sugo de Anatra (fresh pasta with a braised Duck Ragu), Spaghetti con Cozze, Linguine con Gamberi, Orechetti con Salsice, Bucatinni Amatraciana, Rigatoni al Forno, or Cavatappi con Cavalo Fiore alla Schiavelli, and of course my Bolognese.

Every now and then I have to make Schiavelli Pasta for Ada, who is forever harping on me to make it ever since the first time I brought her a plate of it at Caffe Dante one day back in 1999. I got the recipe from a magazine article. It was a story about the actor Vincent Schiavelli who was raised in Brooklyn by his Sicilian grandparents. His grandfather was a Monzu Chef from the town of Polizzi Generosa in Sicily.

The article was about the cookbook Vincent had written about his grandfather and his recipes, and of how he taught Vincent to cook these wonderful old dishes.

One night I made the pasta dish with cauliflower that is in the article (Maccheroni con Cavilofiore). My friend Ada works at New York's most authentic Italian caffe, Caffe Dante on McDougal Street in The Village. Jimmy just so happens to live upstairs from Dante, so whenever we are cooking some food and Ada is not in attendance because she is working, we run a bowl of pasta downstairs to her.

So,one night I made the Pasta with Cauliflower from the magazine article about Vincent Schiavelli and his Old Sicilian Recipes of Polizzi Generosa. Jimmy, Susan, and I ate the pasta along with a bottle of Planeta "Santa Cecilia" from the vineyard of my friend Francesca Planeta. Planeta is one of the rising new stars in Sicilian wine making. The Santa Cecilia (made primarily with Nero d'Avola grapes) was a fine match to the Maccheroni con Cavalo Fiore. It was a quite a nice little meal, and one of the many small, spur of the moment dinners that we decide on that day or the day before. Just three of us having dinner together, sort of like a family meal, not a full blown dinner party, and we make something that is simple, quick, and fast.

A little dinner like this, we usually start with a salad, followed by a Pasta that takes merely twenty to thirty minutes to prepare, and we are set. So of course on this night that I made the Pasta with

100

Cauliflower for the first time, Jimmy ran a plate down to Ada at Caffe Dante. There would be Hell to pay if Ada ever found out that I cooked something and didn't bring any down to her. After the dinner was over and I was leaving Jimmy's place, Ada spotted me heading home. She waved for me to go into the caffe. Well she really went nuts for the Pasta. She loved it and wanted to know what it was called and how I made it. I described the cooking procedure of the dish to her and told her about the magazine article about Mr. Schiavelli. Schiavelli Pasta is not the name of the dish but that is what we call it. Ada and I gave the pasta that name because we like the way it sounds and even more we Love the way it taste. Delicious!

One time when I was still working as a Manager at Da Silvano's, Mr. Schiavelli came into the restaurant. I told him the story about how I had read the article about him in the magazine and how I loved it, and tried some of his recipes. I let him know that my friend Ada who is from Napoli loves the pasta with cauliflower and is constantly begging me to make it for her, and that we named it Schiavelli Pasta after him. Vincent was flattered and quite happy that we liked to cook with his recipes and that we were so fond of them. When he was finished with his dinner at Da Silvano's he wanted to go see Ada at Caffe' Dante. I told him that she didn't work on

Sundays so he didn't go. I haven't seen him since then, but the next time I do, I've been ordered by Ada and Jimmy to invite him to one of our dinners for some wine and a delicious plate of Schiavelli Pasta. Hope he makes it one day. Bravo Vincenzo!!

On December 27, 2003 we held another of our many memorable parties. I had discovered a unique recipe in one of my many cookbooks that I had wanted to make for months. The dish is actually two dishes in one. It's called Anatra en Umido. The way you make the dish is by making a meat sauce that contains ground pork, tomatoes, wine, and aromatic vegetables. You brown a duck (or 2 or more), then let it simmer in the meat sauce for about an-hour-and-a-half until it's cooked through and is tender.

When the duck is finished cooking you serve a pasta course with the sauce that the Duck was braised in, holding back the bird for the next course.

You then serve the Duck as the main course with whatever kind of vegetables that you like. On that particular night, I decided to roast pears with Vin Santo and make braised cabbage to serve with the perfectly cooked Duck. The combination was a phenomenal and everyone present at the Christmas Party flipped for it. Pat Parrotta's girlfriend Gina (now Wife) said that she did not like Duck, but she loved this one. If I must say so, it was rather tasty and quite a big success.

After most of the guests had left and we were just hanging around drinking Campaccio (a Wine my friend Roberto Gundeler makes at his Winery in Radda, Italy), I remarked to Jimmy and Ada, how amazing it was that every single party that we threw, were all so much fun, and utterly successful. The fact that not even one had ever turned out subpar. Every single party has been a huge success filled with fun and lasting memories. These parties are one of the most special parts our lives. We bring people together, and quite simply, we have the most wonderful times imaginable. We cook; we share a meal together, listening to great music, while drinking fantastic Italian wines. We also drink some of the fine wine of cousin Joe Macari makes at his vineyard out on the Eastern end of Long Island, especially one of our favorites, the Collina 48 which goes so well with most of the food we serve as the Wine though made on The North Fork, it is very Italian in style and something both my guests and I appreciate greatly.

If you have the good fortune of being invited to one of the parties of "La Bella Tavola," you must bring a good bottle of wine. We usually like people to bring Italian wine, but we won't shoot you if you bring something else, just don't bring Yellow Tail as someone once did. Italian wines are our favorite, but we do like wines from other countries as well, whether they're from Chile, Spain, Portugal, France, or The United States. We always like a nice Cote du Rhone which I have coined the French version of Chianti.

We usually end up with an excellent array of wines to go along with the meal. We mostly drink Chianti, Barbera, Barolo, Aglianico's, Nero d'Avola, Negroamaro, Brunello, Collina 48, and or Macari's "Bergen Road". We also like Bordeaux's and wines from the Loire Valley of France.

We don't always have dessert, however, most of the time one of the guests brings some cake or pastries or Ada gets some of Caffe Dante's superb Gelato. Often we will get some fresh fruit like a nice juicy Watermelon or Cherries if they are in season. Having fresh fruit at the end of a meal is the norm in Italy, but of course the Italians Love there sweets as well as we do.

Of course great music is always playing at a Bella Tavola party. What's a party without music? Dino, Sinatra, Sammy, The Stones, Dusty Springfield, Nat King Cole, Gato Barbieri, the sounds of Cuba, Brazilian Bossa Nova, Classic Rock, and always plenty of great R & B from the Sixties and Seventies. Jimmy or Ronni like to take care of that aspect of our activities, the Music. No matter which artists we listen to, it is an absolute requirement that we listen to at least three songs from "The Man" himself,

Francis Albert Sinatra. A must! You know there is nothing quite like Frank, Sinatra that is. His music is the perfect accompaniment for our gatherings of friends who fill themselves with tasty Italian Food and Wine, satisfying their senses of site, smell, and taste. The sense of sound is fulfilled with the ultimate of listening pleasures, the sounds of Frank Sinatra, and mingles with conversation amongst friends.The mix always makes for the most festive happy times imaginable. These parties exemplify what a good part of our.lives possess. Yes you do have a good life when you're able to get together with good friends and family, complete with Pasta, Vino, Dolci, e Amore.

"Times spent together at the *Table* with friends and family, are the *Best* times of all!" Breaking Bread, as they say, these are life's truly great pleasures; enjoying food and wine, chatting on conversations of life, relationships, work, and heated political discussions, This–That–and–Every–Other–Thing. You plan trips together. Whether it's a short day or weekend trip to the Hamptons, The North Fork, The Catskill Mountains, or something bigger, like going to Venice, Paris, a Cuban adventure of Rhum, Cigars, and the Sounds of Cuba.

You might plan a food and wine trip through the enchanting Tuscan countryside. We talk about art, literature, and movies while planning what we'll be having for our next meal. We build an amazing battery of special memories that are greater than any type of material things whatsoever.

There is no better way to spend quality time with friends and family than by sitting down at the table, sharing a meal together, whether it's in a restaurant or at home. It's usually better in someone's home, our homes anyway.

Although we may occasionally have other ethnic foods, most frequently it's Italian that we eat at these intimate little banquets of ours. Most of us being Italian, and very proud of our heritage, a heritage which includes; the Music, Wine, and the fabulous Food. It's natural that we eat the food of our ethnic origin. We carry on our Italian Rituals and traditions, making for most happy times. These times started long ago with my Grandparents. The meals and daily rituals continued on with my mother Lucia, her sister Lily, her brothers Frank, Tony, and Jimmy and their children, my cousins, Tony, Phyllis, Joe, Ronni and Mary, Louise, Danna, Allison, Christine, and my brothers Jimmy and Michael, myself, and my sister Barbara. Our Bellino Family Meals took place at my Uncle Jimmy's house on James Street, or at Uncle Tony and Aunt Fran's house in Lodi, The Pleasures of the Table, "La Tavola." The party itself is a recipe that consists of several ingredients that comprise the whole. First of all you need a place to throw the party. Our venue is usually Jimmy Starace's apartment on Macdougal Street in Greenwich Village. To many, if you walked up the five grueling flights of stairs to get the 6th floor and showed them the small one bedroom dwelling and the ten by eighteen foot room that is the combined kitchen and living room and told them that you were going to have a dinner party for twelve to 15 people, they'd think that you've lost your mind. You wouldn't think it would be possible. Thanks to Jimmy, it is. For it wouid never have occurred to me or anybody else for that matter to invite so many people in such a small space, but it works and many have benefited greatly from it. The parties have always been a tremendous success. The success do in part to the ingredients being; a good group of people enjoying each other's company, great Italian Food, chatting about this and that, becoming loose and light from the Wine, while the sounds of Jobim, Sinatra, Dean Martin, Louis Armstrong, Billy Holiday, or Bill Withers play in the background.

It's the kidding around, teasing, and storytelling, bringing people together for good times; the food, the wine, the music, and sharing special moments, that makes the "Perfect Recipe."

I slave over a tiny little stove with hardly any
counterpace to work properly. It's not easy!! But
I Love it. I love the food; to cook it, smell it, share
it, and Eat It with Friends. This is La Bella Tavola.

VEAL PARMIGIANO

Chicken Parmigano,Veal Parmigano, two dishes along with Spaghetti and Meatballs that are both "Greatly Loved" and, ormuch maligned, depending on who you talk to. Some who don'tl ike these dishes and may have negative things to say about them, might be food writers or certain chefs who look down on them as not being real or authentic Italian Cuisine. These people think they know a lot, and they may, but as we all know, nobody knows everything, and there are also differences of opinion to throw into the mix in arguments over who thinks what is actually authentic who has an opposing view.

Meatballs are in fact authentic Italian fare, except that in Italy, they are eaten on their own not with pasta, like we do in America. Not usually.

In and around Sorrento, Italians do eat a dish of Breaded Veal Cutlets with tomato sauce and mozzarella baked on top, however it is not called Veal Parmigano and Italians do not eat nearly as much of this dish as Americans do. Veal Parmigiano and Chicken Parmigiano are much more of an Italian-American thing, along with Spaghetti and Meatballs and other dishes. They are popular with most

Americans and especially those of Italian ancestry. And why not? These dishes are delicious, comforting as well, and regardless of what some say, they have stood the test of time, and in the end, the general public as a whole are the best critics and judges of what is good and what is not, as opposed to a handful of critics with "Bigger Heads" than substance and the proper knowledge to make such statements, or have their opinions carry any weight. I'd say a few million people carry a Hell of a Lot more weight than a handful of under qualified critics with swollen Heads and big egos do. Wouldn't you? Yes, I thought so.

Let us not forget, that food is always evolving, new dishes are created all the time, either on purpose or by accident as was the case with such famous dishes as Fried Ravioli (in St. Louis), Tarte Tatin, Puff Pastry, and a slew of others. Anyone who knows anything about food, knows that food, cuisine, and the foods we eat and what is popular at any given time in history is forever changing. What nobody knows about one day, can well be one of America's or the World's most popular dishes in a matter of a year or two.

Look at Tira mi Su. Before the 80's hardly anyone had ever heard of the dish, even in Italy where it was mainly known of in the region it came from, Venice and the Veneto. As a matter of fact Tira mi Su (Pick me Up) did not become popular in the whole of Italy until after it had first become so insanely popular in the United States. Yes, Tira mi Su was created in Venice, was first popularized in a big way in New York and went on to become a monster hit on Italian Restaurant menus all over the U.S., and then, finally became popular all over Italy. Chicken Parmigiano and Veal Parmigiano are both tasty and satisfying dishes when made properly. Americans love them!

These two dishes are authentic. They are authentic Italian–American Dishes, which is and should be recognized as a legitimate Cuisine, "Cuisine Italian–American,' especially since hundreds of millions of people have eaten and loved these dishes and have validated them through tremendous popularity over the years. They are here to stay, regardless of what their critics say. What do they know anyway?

As anyone with half a brain knows, it is the people, the genral public, the masses who in the end decide. And the masses, the People, the general public just "Love" Italian and Italian–American Cuisne, Chick–Parm, Meatballs, and Veal Parmigiano too!

NEW YORK'S "REAL" LITTLE ITALY

There is a neighborhood in lower Manhattan known as Little Italy. That is the name. Little Italy is an area of New York on many tourists "To Do List."

Tourist's want to go walk around the neighborhood that they think is the most Italian in our fair city. "Far from it!" They want to have a meal, a Cappuccino, and some Dolci Italiano. Now while Little Italy is nice and they do have some great specialty shops there like DiPalo's, Alleva, and Bella Ferrara Bakery; there are a few good restaurants, many so-so, and of course there's Tony's, the Coolest Old Italian bar left in the hood. Little Italy of New York is there for the tourists. There are not many Italian's left living there any longer. There are plenty of Chinese, who seem to be taking over the neighborhood. Anyway, do you want to know where the *real* Little Italy is?

In Manhattan, the area that has the highest concentration of the best Italian restaurants in the city, is the neighborhood that also has the best Italian pastry shops, the best bread bakers, Italian Caffe's, Italian-American Social Clubs, Pork Stores, Pasta Shops, and grocery stores as well as having the highest percenttage of Italian-Americans still living in it? I will tell you the secret. This neighborhood actually comprises two separate pieces of two defined sections of Manhattan. The neighborhood, "The Real Little Italy" happens to be the area that comprises the South-Western part of Greenwich Village as far west as Seventh Avenue, combined with the North-Western part of Soho which used to be part of The Village until it was designated as Soho about forty years or so ago. Anyway the area in question runs roughly from Bleecker Street and Seventh Avenue and goes south to Spring Street from Sixth Avenue on the west side to Thompson Street on its eastern border. In essence, this neighborhood which is "The Real Little Italy" is two pieces of two different parts of Manhattan, Soho and Greenwich Village, a.k.a. the West Village.

It is within these confines, that you will find many people of Italian ancestry still dwelling. They are out on the streets, hanging-out with one-another, playing cards on the Chess Tables at the Spring Street Playground. You'll see some playing stickball or handball, just as they've done for years. After the game, they might get themselves a nice Salami and Provolone Sandwich at Faicco's or pick up a hunk of Mozz (Mozzarella) from Joe's Dairy (this was Jimmy the Cheeseman's shop in The Pope of Greenwich Village), or a Pannino from the "Pannini Nazi" of Soho, Alessandro at Melampo, (a true Italian Pannini Shop on Sullivan Street).

Faicco's, one of the best pork stores in the city is on Bleecker Street at Cornelia. They have all sorts of wonderful imported Cheese from Italy, along with Prosciutto d'Parma and Mortadella from Bologna, Italian made Pasta, Olive Oil, and all sorts of wonderful Italian olives from Sicily, Calabria, and Campagna. Faicco's also make their own Soppressata and fresh Italian Sausages Sweet and Hot, as well as both Beef and Pork Braciole that are ready for cooking. Faicco's also has top quality expertly cut Pork Chops, Steaks, Veal Scallopini, and other cuts of meat from the butcher.

Directly across the street is Zito's Bread which is extremely famous for the excellent bread they've been baking for over 90 years. The West Village and East Village are both historically famous as being the Bread Basket of Manhattan with a good number of Bread Bakers in each neighborhood. Unfortunately these bakeries are disappearing little by little. We have gotten one great new Bread-Baker in recent years, with the "Sullivan Street Bakers" who have come on the scene in a Big Way. They make outstanding Italian and French Bread and are famous for their Ciabatta and Foccacia of which many restaurants use as their House Bread.

Sadly, some of these bakeries are disappearing, as is the case with the First Avenue Bakery which has been replaced with luckily a wonderful Pizzeria in Luzzo's, which has a great décor and some of New York City's best Pizza.

I recently found out that John's Pizzeria was originally a Bread Bakery. One of the Pizzaiolo's at John's was telling me last year that the oven is 120 years old. It was built in 1890, Coal-Fired, and started life as a Oven for baking bread before closing down in 1927. John's was opened as a Pizzeria in 1927 and has been serving the people of Greenwich Village and new York ever since, producing some of the Best Pizza in the country as well as the World. Well at least if you are going to lose something as wonderful as a bakery, getting a Pizzeria instead is not such a bad thing. No loss. And when it comes to such a wonderful place as John's Pizzeria, "Thank You God," for the way things turned out there. We all Love John's.

We lost a famous Bakery that was around the corner from Zito's. Zapperi's was I hear a wonderful Bakery that made Bread, Pastries, Cookies, and all sorts of goodies. There was the bakery on Sullivan Street, on the block of Houston to Prince Streets that was next to Joe's Dairy. It was the Bakery where Pauli in the Pope of Greenwich Village bought his loaf of bread for his sandwich before going to Joe's (Jimmy The Cheeseman's Shop) for Mozzarella and Salami.

Speaking of Zito's, I used to Love walking by late at night and smelling the Bread being baked as I made my way back home after a fun night out. The same holds true of the other famous Italian bread bakers of the neighborhood, Vesuvio's which has been baking delicious bread at the same location on Prince Street for almost 100 years.

On the same block on Bleecker Street as Zito's, you will find two of the finest Italian Pastry Shops in the city. There is Biondi's which was formerly Bleecker Street Pastries, and my favorite, Rocco's. Both pastry shops make a huge array of the most exquisite Cakes, Cookies, and Pastries you could ever want to sink your teeth into. Their wonderful Biscotti, Sfogiatelle, Cannoli, Cheesecakes, Baba Rhum, Lemon Cookies, Pastaciotta, Anisette Toasts, and on and on. The list is too long to mention all the tasty treats at these two delightful establish-ments. Go there and sample as many sumptuous delectable as you can. When it is Christmas Season, you'll find some of the Best Pannettone this side of Italy, baked by Rocco, and around March 19th and Saint Joseph's Day Italian families are able to bring home some tasty St. Joseph's Cake as well. Rocco's is probably the Best Italian Pastry Shop in all New York. You will love it.

Around the corner from these two bakeries you'll find the charming little restaurant Po' where Mario Batali first made his name. Two of his other restaurants Babbo and Lupa are within walking distance from Po' just a few short blocks away. They are within or just out of the neighborhood in question, "New York's Real Little Italy." On the menu at Lupa, you'll find Coda d'Vacinara (Braised Oxtails) and the best Testa (Pigs Head Salami) in town.

Going back down the block from Faicco's, let's get back to John's Pizzeria for a bit more on this fine establishement. For my Money, John's is one of New York's best Pizzas, and the best in Manhattan. The Pizza at John's is cooked to perfection in their famed coal fired oven. There is a wonderful ambiance at John's, especially in the front room where the oven is located, although I do hate the awful looking mural of the Grotto Azzuro that's painted on one wall. The mural looks like the artist stopped painting it before he was even half way finished. It is utterly awful looking, while the Pizza on the other hand is just the opposite, "Utterly Delicious!"

Everybody has their own favorites, like Patsy's up in East Harlem, Totonno's on Neptune Avenue in Coney Island, or Lombardi's on Spring Street. "I do love them all!" John's just happens to be my senti-mental favorite as it was the first *great* pizza I ever tasted. As far as being New York's best, I'm

119

sure Woody Allen would agree. Even before I went to Italy and ate some of the World's best in Napoli and along the Amalfi Coast, I went to John's.

There are two dining rooms at John's, the front one where they make the pizza and a second one called the Woody Allen Room, named after Woody because he used to eat there a lot and shot one of his movie scenes there. The room is not bad, but if you have a choice, take the front room. It is a lot more exciting. You can watch the talented Pizzaiolo at work. These guys are every bit as good as most of the pizza-makers in Old Napoli.

If you walk east on Bleecker to Sixth Ave., make a right, and walk down to the middle of the block, you will come upon two of the most wonderfully authentic Italian restaurants in all of New York City. The very popular Da Silvano and the insanely popular Bar Pitti next door. Both serve, delicious, authentically prepared Tuscan Cuisine in nice casual atmospheres with fun crowds of locals, hipsters, and people in the know. These two restaurants are major celebrity haunts.

Walk into either Restaurant and you're likely to see the likes of such regulars as; Calvin Klein, Sarah Jessica Parker, Gwyneth Palthrow, Uma Thurman, Richard Gere, Anna Wintour, Nick Toshes, Graydon Carter, Keith Richards, Paul McCartney, and David Bowie. Practicaly every Celebrity in the Book, and then there is Silvano Marchetto himself, without a doubt a minor-celebrity in his own right. See if you can understand what he says when if he talks to you. Most people can't. They nod their heads as he banters, pretending they understand his Italian version of "Cousin-It-Like" mumbling. Better get Gomez Adams to translate. It is all part of the show.

Bar Pitti is next to Da Silvano. It is actually an offspring of Da Silvano. Bar Pitti was created by Silvano Marchetto and Giovanni Tognozzi back in 1992, as a cheaper more casual version of Da Silvano. These two fellows have since parted ways. Bar Pitti has blossomed into one of New York's hottest of all Celebrity Haunts and Celeb Seekers frequent the place in droves, in the hopes of maybe rubbing shoulders with Beyonce, Li-Lo, whoever. Bar Pitti is packed Day-and-Night with the Cool, Hip, "In-the-Know" people, and sprinkled with its fair share of Celebs like Lindsay Lohan, Adriana Lima, Julianna Moore, Phillip Seymour Hoffman, and the like. But as hugely popular as Bar Pitti is and for all the Celebs, it's the Food and ambiance that are the Biggest Stars, for Bar Pitti may very well be thee best most consistent Italian Restaurant in all of New York. I kid you not! With wonderful dishes on the menu and tasty Daily Specials with items like; Bolito di Manzo (It's Friggin Awesome), perfect Calves Liver with Butter and Sage, Paparadell con

Sugo di Coniglio, the tastiest most succulent Oxtails in town, and a host of all sorts of phenomenal plates. You'll Love it.

Walk down the block to Houston, make a left walking around the playground, and another left when you get to McDougal Street and you'll find Villa Mosconi, a fine restaurant that makes excellent straight-forward Italian Food cooked by a actual real Italian Chef who was born in Italy in Emilia Romagna. Chef Pietro Mosconi immigrated to New York with his father in the late 1960's and opened Villa Mosconi in 1976 and has been cooking some of Greenwich Village's and New York's best and most authentic Italian Food ever since. One block north, also on Macdougal Street is Villa Mosconi's sister restaurant Monte's which the Mosconi Family opened in 1983, so you'll see Chef Pietro in either Monte's, Villa Mosconi or meandering somewhere along the one block stretch between his two wonderful restaurants.

Pietro, his family and their two restaurants are just one of many happy Italian-American success stories of Greenwich Village and New York's "Real Little Italy."

Next door to Villa Mosconi is Tiro a Segno, a Private Italian-American Gun Club where Chef Giovanni makes some of the Best Italian Food to be found in New York. However most will never taste it, as Tiro a Segno is a private club. The Club is the Oldest Italian-American Club in the country, where you can mingle with fellow Italian Americans, with an Apertivo at the Bar of Campari or Aperol before proceeding into the dining room to sit for a mouth watering meal cooked by Giovanni and his more than cable crew.

After dinner, a waiter or Captain will ask you if you would like to go downstairs to do a little shooting at the Gun-Range in the basement. It's quite a lot of fun, so if you're not a member, see if you can make friends with someone who can get you in, for one of the many special events like an Italian Easter Dinner or Wild Game Dinner and the ever popular Truffle Night held every year come Autum and the start of White Truffle Season. You will have the time of your Life if you are able to plot your way in.

Right next to Tiro a Segno, which by the way means "Shoot a Leg" in Italian, is Caffe Dante, quite possibly the best Italian Caffe in all of New York. No check that, Caffe Dante "Is" thee Best Italian Caffe in all New York, Bar None.

Leaving Caffe Dante, make a left and walk up McDougal crossing Bleecker Street and passing by Monte's you'll come upon Caffe' Reggio. This caffe' has a marvelous ambiance, filled with antiques and beautiful old paintings, with quite a lot of History, including a bench that came from a Medici Palazzo in

Florence. It dates back to the Renaissance, and they have a spectacular painting that comes from a painter of the School of Caravaggio. Caffe' Reggio opened its doors in 1927 and to be not only New York's oldest caffe, but the oldest in the country.

I have to mention Rocco's Restaurant on Thompson Street. Rocco's is wonderful, and is just one of a small handful of true old "Old School Italian Restaurants" left in the West Village. There are still two remaining in the East Village, with John's on East 12th Street and Lanza's just a couple blocks away on 1st Avenue between East 10th and Eleventh Streets. Both of these restaurants have recently turned 100 Years Old and in the case of John's, pretty much nothing has changed and you can still see the 100 Year Old Tile Floors, Bar, and Murals of Venice, The Bay of Naples, and other Italian Scenes. Lanza's was still the same until the current owners messed things up by taking down the dividing archway, removing the old refrigerated showcase, adding a Bar and putting up wainscoting. They've ruined the place, but the old original murals remain.

Back to Rocco's on Thompson Street in Greenwich Village. Rocco's is not nearly as old as John's or Lanza's but it is old enough and has the delightful Old School New York Italian Restaurant feel, complete with the Old School once insanely prevalent American Italian Restaurant Menu with dishes like Baked Clams Oreganata, Clams Casino, Fried Calamari, Stuffed Mushrooms, Mussels or Clams Posillipo, Linguini with White or Red Clam Sauce, Fettucine Alfredo, Chicken and Veal Parmigiano. There's alsoChicken or Veal Francese, Veal Marsala, and Gamberoni Piacere, translated to Shrimps in any sauce you like, such as; Shrimp Scampi, Shrimp Parmigiano, or Shrimp Fra d'Avlo. "Now, can You beat that?" No! You just gotta Love a restaurant that's Old School Italian, has the old ambiance, and makes all those delicious old dishes that millions know and Love.

As I've stated before, and many of you know, there was a time when most Italian Restaurants in the U.S. had that same typical Cookie Cutter Italian Menu of a lot of dishes with Red Sauce and Mozzarella baked on top. In the early 80's people started opening restaurants that began doing away with the old cliché dishes. They started serving new more authentic Italian Food on their menus.

Many had come to look down on these Old School Cliché Italian American dishes. I'm sorryto say that I was one of them. I was making my kitchen bones and I was all about Italy and cooking the most authentic Italian Food possible. I had started going to Italy every year, and I could see things were a bit different. I knew what real authentic Italian Food was. I began to openly speak out against things like

Spaghetti and Meatballs and Chicken Parmigiano, though I still loved them and would Secretly eat them on the sly. I was too young and inexperienced, though I didn't think so at the time. I had been to Italy a couple times and thought I knew it all. Or if not know it all, that I knew a lot and more than most, which was true. What I didn't know, was that though it was good to know and study authentic Italian Food that is made in Italy, the fact was that throughout history, food and new cuisines evolve. Things change and new cuisines are created. What I didn't know and millions of others for that matter, was that Italian-American Food is a viable cuisine. It is a cuisine that has ev-olved from Italian Food of Italian Immigrants to America, beginning just before 1900, and growingin the 20's, 30's, 50's, and 60's. This New Cuisine, Italian-American is based on Italian Food as it was made by immigrants from Italy to the United States and later their descendants who love and make the food their parents, grandparents, aunts, and uncles made.

Yes, dishes like Chicken Parmigiano and Veal Francese are not authentically Italian Food from Italy, what there are, are dishes that are of the Italian-American Cuisine created by both Italians born in Italy who moved to America, their children and grandchildren. Italian-American Food, is real, it's a cuisine of its own, and it is viable.

Now, back to Greenwich Village/Soho and the Real Little Italy, complete with Italian-Americans and "Real Italian-American Food."

If you go down to Sullivan Street just above Spring Street you will find Alesandro, the owner of Melampo, a great little shop where you can get some awesome tasting Pannini. Alessandro is known by many as the "Pannini Nazi." Alessandro's little Pannini Shop "Melampo" is next to the Blue Ribbon and the Spring Street Playground, where you can still see old Italian men and ladies hanging-out playing cards on the sidewalks and chit-chatting about this-that and every-other-thing. Alessandros' shop is small. He just sells Italian san-dwiches and beverages to go. His pannini shop was probably the first. There are a slew of them all over the city now, but Alessandro has them beat by a good dozen years or so. This little shop is quite famous for its tasty Sandwiches, but is also known for the quirky character of Alessandro, the so called "Pannini Nazi" in reference to the famed "Soup Nazi" from the Seinfield TV Show and fame.

Alessandro has a menu of sandwiches with names like Trombino, Parma, and Napoletana. There are all sorts of variations of sandwiches of Prosciutto, Soppressata Mortadella, roast peppers, Caponata, Mozzarella, Provolone, and other items. You *must* order by the name of the sandwich and there can be no deviations. If you are allergic to cheese like a friend of mine is, it's just 'Too Dam Bad," as far as Alessandro is concerned. You are not allowed to order a sandwich from the menu that has cheese on it and ask Alessandro to, "Hold the Cheese, please." He does not like this. "No changes!" That's the law of Alessandro. If you ask for a change, he'll snap, "Just what's on the menu." Don't answer him back or he'll throw you out of his shop, lickity split as I've witnessed on a couple of occasions. It's pretty funny.

His store is a mere 12 feet by 18 feet and he is the only one there. He does not have anybody working with him and sometimes he gets backed up when it gets a little busy. Sometimes you have to wait on a line that goes out the door onto Sullivan Street. Make sure you don't make the mistake of getting antsy and making some sort of remark as to why things are taking so long, Alessandro will throw you out on your Ass, you might even be "Banned for Life." Did I mention that the sandwiches are great? People like Martin Scorsesee, Roberto Biannini, and the late great Marcello Mastrianni have been subject to the wrath of Alessandro, just to eat one of his little masterpieces. And that's why he won't let you make any changes. He's a "Temperamental Artist." He views himself this way, and his Pannini as Little Pieces of Art. The bread is the canvas and the

Salami, Provolone, Prosciutto, and other ingredients are the paints that he makes his creations with.

Back track on Sullivan Street north and you'll come to Joe's Dairy. This is the spot where you can get "Thee Best Mozzarella" in town. Joe's is a tiny little shop that makes Fresh Mozzarella and Smoked Mozzarella every day. You can also get Imported Italian Salumi and Cheeses such as Parmigiano Reggiano and Prosciutto d' Parma, but it's Joe's Fresh Mozzarella that's the Star, and you won't find better "Mozz" anywhere.

Across from Joe's is Pino's Italian Butcher Shop, and walk across Houston Street to the 100 Year Old Pasta Shop Raffetto's for some great fresh Cheese or Meat Ravioli, Fettuccine, Paparadelle, and a whole slew of Pastas.

So, there you have it. This area is the true Little Italy in reality if not in name. There are great caffe's as well as the largest concentration of some of the city's best Italian Restaurants, Caffes, Pork Stores, Pizzerias, Bakeries, Italians, and Italian-American living. If you're visiting on vacation, you now know a few secrets that few tourists never will. Check it out. Both the Real Little Italy, and the touristy one on Mulberry Sreet and you decide which you like better.

A PICNIC in CENTRAL PARK

One of the many things thatNew Yorkers are blessed with is Central Park. Central park is Beautiful, it's Wondrous, it's a gift, a gift from another generation that, Thank God was smart and foresighted enough to set aside a large track of land and give New Yorkers the World's most Beautiful and Magnificent of City Parks. Of all the parks in cities around the World and there are many great one's like; The Borghese Gardens in Rome, Luxenbourg Garden in Paris, Mont Royal Park in Montreal, The Boston Commons in Boston, and a host of others, it is New York's Central Park which is not only the most famous, and to be quite blunt, thee best. It's absolutely beautiful and its diversity, size, and usefulness to both locals and tourist is without compare. Central Park is massive. It stretches from 59th Street on its most southern border and ends way up on 107th Street in the north. It's bigger than the country of Monaco! It is filled with paths, ponds, a lake, a reservoir, a gigantic swimming pool, a huge ice skating rink, tennis courts, bridle trails, numerous baseball diamonds, volley ball courts, a roller–skating area, a zoo, formal gardens, a Carousel, band shells, fountains, The Delacorte Theatre, woods, The Sheep Meadow, and The Great Lawn.

This beautiful Park with all its vegetation, trees, flowers, lawns, gardens, and shrubbery is the most perfect place for a picnic in the city.

Going to Central Park is a great way to escape all the concrete, steel, and blacktop within the concrete jungle itself. A picnic in the park is an excellent way to spend time with a group of friends, and it's an extremely romantic thing to do with that special someone of yours. I did this a few times with my Ex-Girlfriend Isabel. I'd pick up a nice bottle of wine (Chianti), Prosciutto, a couple different types of Cheese; maybe some Manchego (Isabel's favorite), and some Pecorino Toscano. I'd buy some Apples and Grapes, and make a tasty Sausage and Pepper Frittata, some of my famed Caponata, and presto-chango you've got the perfect Italian Picnic.

I have a nice woven Old-Time Picnic Basket that I'd pack all the goodies in, and we'd be set. Don't forget the Swiss Army knife and the corkscrew, or the Swiss Army Knife with corkscrew, and?

We'd go over to the Gazebo that is on the on the lake near 79th, "A most beautiful and romantic spot." Isabel and I would lay everything out. I'd open the bottle of wine and we'd nosh, chat, and smooch. For any of you guys out there who are a bit short in the Romance department, try doing this for your girl sometime. You will score major points as I always have. Just about any woman in the World would concure and dream of having this done for her. Do it for your girl. Your wife, or some lady you're trying to score points with, this treatment and jesture will put you on the tiop of her list. She'll Love it! She'll adore you for it, and you will both benefit greatly from such a memorable experience. The times Isabel and I had there, having those picnics were indescribably beautiful. They bring back fond memories of Isabel and the relationship we once had.

I have also had a few picnics in Central Park with small groups of friends besides those romantic interludes with Isabel. My good friend Andrew and his former wife Cappy and I had a really nice one a few years back. We had some nice Bordeaux wines that they both liked so much. We procured some good cheese, fresh fruit, a couple baguettes, and some homemade Caponata that the two of them pleaded with me to make for the picnic. They Love It, much. We brought a cassette player ("remember those things?") to play some Tony Bennett and Sinatra, my favorites and of Andy and Cappy as well. The time we had in Central Park that day w as a special one that we still talk about to this very day. A picnic in Central Park. Central Park is amazing. It is always there, so "Do It," a Picnic in Central Park.

The MACARI FAMILY VINEYARD

What could be better than a Summertime lunch on a beautiful vineyard among the vines? Summertime dinner?

It is my great fortune to have a cousin who owns one of the most beautiful vineyards on the North Fork of Long Island. Joe Macari Jr. and Joe Macari Sr. are the proprietors of a vineyard that produces some of the finest examples of North Fork wine with their famed Bordeaux Blend Style wine Bergen Road, Sauvignon Blanc "Katherine's Field," a serious single- varietal Cabernet Franc and the hugely popular desert wine "Block E," made from Sauvignon Blanc, Chardonnay, and Viognier grapes. The wine is literally a Nectar of the Gods. No exageration!

Over the years we have had some incredible meals there. We have had the sort of lunches, dinners, picnics, and get-togethers that most people could only dream of. We grill whole Filets of Beef and succulent Porterhouse Steaks, braise rabbits, and roast whole goats and Baby Lamb. We make amazing Pizza in Joe's wood burning Italian Pizza Oven, along with Focaccia, and all sorts of Italian goodies.

A meal can be as simple as throwing some Hot and Sweet Italian Sausages on the grill with some onions to be served on a loaf of crusty Italian Bread.

Now since Joe bought a beautiful Berkel Slicer, a quick meal can be even simpler than the Sausage and Pepper Sandwiches. Joe usually has a leg of Prosciutto di Parma and some sort of Salami on hand, so all we have to do is pick up some bread, throw the Prosciutto onto the Berkel, and slice away. Put some salami on the sandwich with a few slices of Fresh Mozzarella or slices of tomato, and you are set. You have got a sandwich fit for a King. On the other hand we may make full-scale Italian meals consisting of an array of mixed antipasti of roast peppers, Sicilian Olives, Cacitorini, asparagus, and frittata followed by a bowl of pasta. The main course might be a whole Roast Bass, a Roast Leg of Lamb, or a mixed grill of chicken, Sausage, and sliced Sirloin of Beef.

The best thing about cooking out at the vineyard is that we often get the most amazing fresh fish. My young cousins Tommy, Joey, and Edward are avid fishermen. They often bring back a nice catch of Bluefish, Flounder, Sea Bass, and Porgies. One time the boys were in a Fluke Fishing Tournament for a whole weekend. The boys caught about thirty pounds of the most beautiful freshest fish imagineable.

One night, I just breaded and fried up the pristine filets of Fluke. I made my famous Potato and Chive Salad, Kit Macari cooked some tasty fresh Spring Asparagus with Parmigiano and breadcrumbs, and I made some Slow Roast Plum Tomatoes, along with a mixed green salad. Cousin Joe cracked open a bottle of Macari Sauvignon Blanc 2003, as well as a magnum bottle of Marchese Antinori Chianti Classico Riserva 1997 and we were set. The meal was incredible. In the whole wide World, you would not have been able to eat better than we ate that night at Macari Vineyards. The wines were great; Macari Sauvignon Blanc was a perfect accompaniment to the Fluke. It was nice, clean and crispy with grassiness and Gooseberries in the palate. The Marchese Antinori that we drank was phenomenal. A great wine, to say the least, it had aged nicely, was nicely balanced with taste Sour Cherries in the palate, with just a touch of spice. It was a most enjoyable wine.

The next night we cooked more Fluke. This time we made a nice fish stew with the Fluke, some Mussels, Tomatoes, Garlic, Onions, Potato, with Saffron, and fresh thyme from Alexandra Macari's garden. We drank a couple bottles of the Macari Estate Chardon-nay with the North Fork Fish Stew that we made, and all was fine in our World.

So, for anyone who loves to eat fish, there is nothing quite like eating fish that was pulled out of the water just a few short hours before you eat it. More than any other food item, you want to know that your fish is super fresh, so to be able to get it like that, this is unbeatable. Besides the boys bringing back some great fresh catches, quite often we have bestowed upon us, freshly caught fish from any number of friends who drop off a part of their fresh catch as well. When you get fresh fish like that, the best way to cook it is in the simplest manner possible. We usually just season the fish with Salt and Pepper and either grill, roast, or sauté them in a little butter and olive oil and sprinkle on some fresh lemon and chopped parsley. "Voila!!! You're not going to eat better fish anywhere!" To go along with the fish we might have a nice mélange of vegetables that one of the neighbors dropped off from their garden. Things like zucchini, green beans, fava, and nice ripe tomatoes.

One time I made some Fish Tacos with some fresh haddock that the boys caught. I had recently read a magazine article about the famous Fish Tacos of the Baja Peninsula of Mexico and I was dying to make them. When little Joey, Edward, and Tommy brought those fresh filets of Haddock home and Alex asked me how we should cook them, I knew exactly what to do.

Alexandra Macari is one of my favorite cooking partners. She is forever pulling things out of the cupboard and telling me, "Throw this in Danny, throw this in too. Let's use these carrots," etc., etc.. We always have a lot of fun in the kitchen, where the rewards are always great; Fresh Fish, Wine, Pasta, Salumi, Bolognese, fresh local vegetables, and-on- and-on.

The lasttime I was there, Joe Macari Sr. cooked up some fine Salmon Steaks and a whole Filet of Beef on the grill. The dinner was awesome.

Let us not forget the gorgeous setting of the vineyard which is 500 acres that starts on Sound Avenue in Mattituck and stretches up to the Long Island Sound itself. The vineyard is planted with 170 acres of vines of Merlot, Chardonnay, Viognier, Cabernet Sauvignon, Malbec, Syrah, Cabernet Franc, Pinot Noir, Sauvignon Blanc, and Petite Verdot.

Joe has a beautiful herd of Texas Long Horns, Herford, and Black Angus Cattle. Along with the Big Bull "Mr. Widespread," Joe has three Sicilian Donkeys, Horses, Chickens, Turkeys, and Goats.

Besides the farm animals; rabbits, quail, fox, and deer run wild through the vineyard. This makes for a unbelievable setting for a meal, drinking the wines from Macari Family Vineyards, along with incrediable wines from Italy, France, Spain, and Argentina.

"Who could ask for more?"

DO DON'TS CHOPSTICKS & SPOONS

There are certain things about eating in Italy, in Italian restaurants in New York, or trying to recreate the most authentic experience when cooking and eating Italian Food at home. Things one should know and adhere to. Here is some information that you can do with whatever you'd like. For example; I am aware that Italians do not drink Cappuccino any time after twelve noon. In Italy, Cappuccino is only for breakfast and Italians in Italy only drink it in the morning. They make fun of Americans who drink it in restaurants and caffes in Italy in the afternoon and evenings after dinner. Cappuccino, according to the Italians, is for breakfast, and in the morning only, but try telling that to tens of millions of Americans who drink it morning, noon, and night, each and every day. Try telling them they can only have it in the morning and not at any other time of the day. As those big burly Italian guys who wear big burly Pinky Rings would say, "Fuggetabout-it!"

Also. Italians do not serve Espresso with a lemon peel. That's an Italian American thing. Try telling Americans they can't do that as well, especially those Big Burly Guys with Pinky Rings. Working in the restaurant business for years, I've had to tell people who ask for lemon peel with their espresso, that it is not proper to do so. You never serve a lemon peel with espresso in Italy. Never, ever. They look at you like you've got three heads. It's not really a big deal, but if you want to do as the Italians do, you'll omit the peel.

Another thing, when you're in a restaurant it's not really proper to eat your spaghetti or other long pasta with a tablespoon as well as the fork. You just use a fork. Don't ask the waiter for a spoon. The spoon thing is an American thing, not Italian, and it's funny, as most Americans think they are eating Pasta in the proper Italian way. "Not." A spoon is for Soup, unless you're in Thailand, where their utensils are a Fork and Spoon, no Knife, and "No Chopsticks."

Do you hear me? No Chopsticks. Thai people do not use Chopsticks to eat. Never have. This is an American Thing, though Americans think they are doing as the Thais do when eating with Chopsticks. "Not."

In Italy Pasta is a course of its own, not a side dish, so don't expect a side of Spaghetti with your Veal Milanese in Italy. Though in the United States, some Italian restaurants may or may not give you a side of Spaghetti or some other pasta with your Entrée, free of charge or not. As some Italian restaurants in the U.S. that want to adhere strictly to the Italian way and not Italian–American way, they probably won't serve a side of pasta with your main course, and if you insist on having a side order of Spaghetti Pomodoro with your Chicken, Meat, or Fish dish, they will charge you for it. You need to know where you are and what the way that particularlocal. There are still Old Style Italian American restaurants around that automatically serve all entrees with a side of Pasta or they'll let you havea choice between a side of some sort of Pasta (Spaghetti, Penne, or Ziti with Tomato) or a vegetable.

If you want a side of Pasta with your Entrée and you don't want to be charged for it, you need to be in one of these places that does so.

Grated Cheese? Parmigiano, Grana, or Pecorino? Just because you are in an Italian Restaurant, it doesn't mean that grated cheese goes on top of everything on the menu. Certain pasta dishes depending on what the sauce is may or may not have cheese grated on them. Most do, in fact, but not everything, especially not on Vongole (Clam Sauce) or any Pasta that has Seafood in the sauce. It just doesn't get Grated Cheese on top, especially Spaghetti Vongole. It sacrilegious, so "Don't ask for grated cheese on your Linguine with Clam

142

Sauce. "Just don't do it!!" Unless maybe you want to go to the prison."

Hey, I used to be really hard core on things like this and would strictly adhere to the Italian (Italian, not Italian-American) way. I've gotten lenient on these hard and fast Rules. Hey if you want Grated Cheese on top of your Spaghetti Vongole, go right ahead. If you want to ruin a perfectly balanced dish of Spaghetti (or Linguine) with Garlic, Olive Oil, Peperincino, Fresh Parsley, and lovely fresh little Clams with . their delicate taste of which would be ruined and overpowered by the Cheese, by all means, go right ahead! Why should I care? Just Kidding. I'm really not as Hard-Core as I used to be on these subjects, and especially that I know, realize, and advocate the fact that Italian-American Cuisines a viable one, and based on the Italian Food and Cuisine of the Mother-Country Italy, there are some slight variations here and there, and it is these variations that make the food Italian-American and not the Italian Cuisine and Food of Italy itself. All perfectly fine. Snobs and "Know-It-Alls" who think they know everything, but really do not, need to grasp on to the fact that the food of Italian-America is a real and viable Cuisine, these facts have been proven over many years by 10's of Millions of Americans, of Italian origin and otherwise.

Now, if you happen to be in Italy and want vegetables with your main course (secondo), you may have
to order whatever vegetable (Contorno) you'd like
on the side. It is proper to eat vegetables with your
main course; it's just that in Italy if you want the
vegetables, they do not automatically put vegetables
on the plate with the main course as we do in
America. You have to order them on the side. In
most restaurants they don't put them on the plate
with the fish, meat, or poultry. That's just the way
they do it. Mainly because you may have had a
good amount of vegetables already in the courses
preceding the main course (Secondi) and you might
not need more vegetables. If you do, you order them
as a Contorni, meaning conture to the main item,
the meat, poultry, or fish on the plate as main course.

Do not be surprised if you're in Italy and you
hardly ever see Cheesecake on the restaurant menus.
Italians do eat cheesecake, but not very often, not as
much as Italian-Americans do, though the percep-
tion of most Americans is that Italian do eat a lot of
Cheesecake. Even in New York, not as many Italian
restaurants serve Cheesecake anymore, not as much
as they used to, nor Tortoni, or Spumoni as more
than 90% of restaurants used to do in the by gone
days of old Italian Red Sauce Restaurants. I'll tell
you though, I do miss Tortoni (Vanilla Ice Cream

with Toasted Almonds on Top). Yummm! Wish Tortoni would make a bit of a comeback. I miss that tasty old dessert, that as a kid, was always a Special Treat whenever we could get one.

If you're in Italy and see Spaghetti and Meatballs on the menu of some restaurant, turn around and get out of there but quick. That's a restaurant catering to the tourist crowd, and the food is probably not very good. There are a few of these restaurants in around Italy, especially in heavily trafficked tourist areas in Rome, Florence, and Venice. If you're looking for a nice authentic meal in Italy, learn the telltale signs. It's not that difficult.

Don't get me wrong, being Italian–American I love Spaghetti and Meatballs (and if I see them on a Menu in America where I know they're good, I'll get them). It's just that if you see them on a menu in a restaurant in Italy, there is something wrong. It's a tourist restaurant, and if you're looking for a real Italian meal you'll probably be better off going elsewhere. They do not serve butter or olive oil with the bread in Italy. They will give it to you if you ask, because they know that Americans like it, but it is not the Italian way.

If you want to have a full Italian Style Meal of Italy, it consists of at least three courses. The most popular three course meal starts with Antipasto (appetizers), then Primo Piatto (Pasta, Risotto, or Soup), and Secondo (the main course). Italians do not eat dessert that much. Sometimes they do, but mostly they will have fruit or cheese at the end of the meal. They might have a Grappa, a Digestivo, or a dessert wine like Vin Santo or Passito de Pantelleria.

If you'd like to have a nice festive meal that is an all day affair, like the ones my family would have over my Aunt Fran's house, you should serve at least four courses spread out over three to five hours. You begin with some sort of Antipasto platters that are served family style, then you'll have a pasta or soup course, the main course, and once you make it to the dessert course, this is longest, drinking Coffee, munching on a large array or pastries, cookies, and cakes, some Anisette and lots of long heated discussions, chit-chat, and local and International Gossip. The dessert course can take three hours or more before people start heading home. A good time had by all.

So, all this being said, remember, Italian-American Cuisine is "Yes" a Real Full-Fledged Cuisine, a few Hundred Million people have proven this over many years. Dishes like Spaghetti and Meatballs, Baked Clams, Chicken Parmigiano are delicious when pre pared properly. That's why they have been eaten and orderd Hundreds of Millions of times in

Italian-American Restaurants over the years.

Remember, Italian-America is Italian-American and Italian-American Food, Italy is Italy, and Italian Food, so, "when in Rome?" "You know what to do," Eat as the Romans do, and in Brooklyn?

TONY'S

There's an old Italian Bar in New York City called Tony's Nut House. That's the nickname. I won't tell youthe real name, and I will not tell you exactly where it is. Some will know, and if you are determined to go there, you'll have to do a little foot work.

Tony's is one of those great old bars of New York, discovering it thrills and excites. On discovery, you become ecstatic and stunned the place still exist. "Thank God," its great charm and uniqueness preserved. There are far too few of these cool old relics left. This is why I will not divulge the name, nor the location. If you really want to go, you'll find it.

There still remains a precious few other old joints like Tony's. There's Pete's Tavern and The Old Towne Bar, both in Gramercy Park, McSorley's on East 7th Street, Peter McManus in Chelsea, Milano's on Houston Street, PJ Clarkes up on Third Avenue, and Fanelli's in Soho.

The two greatest things about Tony's is the wonderful old décor, the same and unchanged for some 80 years, and of course there's Tony the man himself. Tony is a cool old Italian guy with a great "I don't give a Shit," attitude. He doesn't say much, he doles out drinks, and when he's not busy serving, he sits at a bar stool with a big old stogey in his mouth and a remote control in his hand. There's a great picture of him behind the bar with The Chairman of the Board, "Francis Albert Sinatra." There's also a great picture of him with Madonna and one with Ronald Reagan. There have been a number of movies that have had scenes shot in Tony's. They shot some scenes from State of Grace, The Pope of Greenwich Village (in which Tony played himself), Donny Brasco, The Godfather III, as well as some sit-downs in the Soprano's. Tony likes having movies shot at his place and he enjoys the notoriety.

You won't find any fancy drinks, ATM'S, or pinball machines at Tony's. You will find a great Old World drinking-mans-bar with authentic wear worn décor and a truly grand Barkeep in Tony. There's a jukebox filled with Sinatra, Dean Martin, Tony Bennett, Jerry Vale, The Rolling Stones, and good old R&B. Thank God there's not an ounce of Rap, Heavy Metal, or Techno, "Tony wouldn't *tolerate* that kind of *CRAP*." Is there anything more one could ask for? Maybe the greatest little bit of restroom wall poetry you're likely to ever encounter? Something one of Tony's buddies undoubtedly wrote and I stumbled across one day as I was in the men's room using the facilities. I was washing my hands when I noticed it. A little bit of scripture on the bathroom walls, a threat to those who write and mess up the Mens Room Walls at Tony's place. It read, and I quote, "Stop Writtin on Tony's Walls You Prick!!!" How's that for good old unadulterated Working-Class New York Prose?

EASTER SUNDAY "BUONA PASQUA"

In the year 2003 I was lucky enough to spend Easter Sunday with all my Aunts and Uncles at Uncle Tony's house in Lodi, needless to say, that dinner as all dinners of Aunt Fran and Uncle Tony's house were always great. The dinner brought back many fine memories of all the family dinners of days gone by, of splendid times spent with brother and sister, Mom and Dad, Aunts, Uncles, and Cousins.

Yes I have a lifetime of remembrances from that house of my mother's brother Tony, where the entire family gathered for many a tasty meal. Meals filled with Antipasti, Ravioli, Pasta and Peas, Sausages, Meatballs, Coffee, Cannoli, and heated chatter of all sorts, of; Sports, local gossip, gossip of the news, including Joey Buttafuoco, Congressional indiscretions, what-ever. The conversation is always led by Uncle Frank.

These Sunday get-togethers of my childhood were attended by my mother's sister and brothers families. Well on this particular Easter Sunday of 2003 none of my cousins were there. The party consisted of Uncle Frank, Aunt Helen, Aunt Wanda, Aunt Fran, Uncle Tony, and me. My brother Jimmy stopped by for a little visit. He said he didn't want anything to eat as he was going to dinner at his wife's sister's house. Jimmy then proceeded to woof down a large plate of Ravioli, Sausage, and Meatballs, just a little snack to hold him over to his other dinner. "Ha-ha."

Our dinner consisted of a simple tossed salad of lettuce, tomato, and Cucumbers dressed with Salt, pepper, Red Wine Vinegar, and Olive Oil. We followed the salad with Ravioli's from a local Italian specialty shop in Garfield. The Ravioli's were served with some Sunday sauce that Aunt Helen had made with Sausage, Meatballs, and Braciola. Aunt Helen's Meatballs are the best! When they are around, it's hard to stop eating them. I had about seven of them that day and took some home with me to make a Meatball Parm Sandwich for lunch the next day, Meatball Parm Mondays. I asked Aunt Helen how she makes her Meatballs. "I use Veal, Pork, and Beef and I make the butcher put the meat through the grinder three times." Wow, you have to know the butcher pretty well to get him to put the meat through that many times, but I guess Aunt Helen has her connections. "I put in some onions, a little garlic, parsley, and some Pecorino. That's my secret darling," she told me. It goes without saying that the course with the Sunday Sauce was fantastic. Aunt Fran and Uncle Tony made the main course number two, a Baked Ham complete with Fresh Pineapple. Can you believe that? Not one, but two main courses!

Hey, it's a special day, it's easter Sunday. Yes, I know tha Lamb is the most traditional meat, or any food item to eat for that matter for Easter Sunday, but it seems as though my mother, her sister Lilly, and her bothers Frank, Tony, and James didn't go for lamb that much, thus the Sunday Sauce, Pasta, and Baked ham on the Sunday. "Hey, I'm not gonna complain, nothing is better than Sunday Sauce, especially one made by Aunt Hellen.

So, Uncle Tony made some tasty Sweet Potatoes, another of my favorites. Love those Sweet Potatoes!! So does Uncle Tony, that's why he makes them, and because our Uncle Frank likes them as well. Green Beans were also served, along with some Kernel Corn, another favorite of both Uncle Frank and Uncle Tony. The Sweet Potatoes and Ham were both quite tasty. They make the best food; Aunt Helen, Uncle Tony, and Aunt Fran. We all know that by now, don't we?

With dinner we drank some Ruffino Chianti and my uncle's favorite, Carlo Rossi Paesano. I love that wine. It's cheap jug wine made by Italian-Americans in California, (many would look down on it in disdain) but it's wine we grew up with along with Gallo Hearty Burgundy. Along with millions of other Italian Americans, we had a special way to drink wine from the jug whereby you stick your index finger through the little handle as you place the main body of the jug on your forearm, you bring the opening to your mouth while swiveling your arm upward so the wine flows into your mouth. It's a great old Italian-American tradition.

I will never forget the first time, many years ago, when my Uncles Tony and Frank showed my cousin Anthony and I how to do this properly. My cousin Tony grabbed the jug first to give it a shot. Then I did it. We both loved it! That simple act is still to this very day, quite vivid in my mind. It is amazing how the smallest things mean so much. I guess it wasn't just the act of drinking the wine from the handled jug but the fact that we were with people who we loved; Uncles Frankie and Tony, cousin Tony and Aunt Fran. The Family, La Famiglia! That's what made it so special. Imagine that this little event still brings back such wonderful memories. Still to this very day. It is truly amazing.

For dessert, Aunt Fran made Ricotta Cookies that were Out-of This-World!!! The Ricotta Cookies were spectacular. I had never had them before and as with the Meatballs, I couldn't stop munching on them for the rest of the day. I must have had a dozen or more. Aunt Helen made some tasty treats as well; Sesame Cookies and Almond Crescents. We had some Anisette with our dessert, along with Espresso that Aunt Helen made in her Napoletana. A Napoletana is a two-piece pot that you make Espresso in. You put water in the bottom part, the ground coffee goes in a compartment in the middle and you screw the top on. You place the pot over a flame on the stove. When the water comes to a boil, you take the pot off, turn it upside-down and wait for the boiling water to flow through the ground coffee, making a nice pot of Espresso, every time.

I always loved those Napoletana coffee pots and bought one for myself the first time I was in Napoli. I also love to bring back the beautiful ceramics they make in the little seaside town of Vietro Sul Mare. Whenever I'm down on the Amalfi Coast I pick up a few of those lovely plates. I've now accumulated quite a nice collection of plates, bowls, and water jugs that I serve my home-cooked meals on. These plates only add to an already wonderful experience of cooking and eating our tasty home-cooked Italian dishes.

Using as many products as we can that are from Italy, such as Olive Oil, Pasta, Vinegar, Cheese, Olives, and such, just adds to the experience, and of course the wine; Chianti, Sicilian Nero d'Avola, Sal-ice Salentino, Brunello, combined with those of Italian-Americans of The Gallo's, Carlo Rossi, The Italian-American Wine Royalty of The Mondavi's, and Macari Vineyards.

Along with the coffee and desert, one of the highlights of any Bellino Family meal is hearty conversation, always led by our "Leader," Uncle Frank. I was able to get Uncle Frank, Uncle Tony, and my aunts to tell some stories which I recorded for prosperity on video tape. Aunt Helen and Fran wrote down a few of their recipes for me. Gotta make those cookies.

Easter Sunday with the Aunts and Uncles is always a special time. This one was no different, and another to add to the memories of many gone by.

The TURKEY TURNED to VENISON

One year, not too long ago, I was finally able to accept an invitation to Thanksgiving dinner at the house of my very good friends James and Ann Starace. I had been invited many times, but I usually celebrate Turkey Day with some family members.
So this year, it was out to Staten Island for Thanksgiving at the Starace's, Staten Island Italian-American Style.

The plan was to meet at Caffe Dante to assemble everyone for the trip out to that other Bourough. Making the trip for the Thanksgiving dinner were; myself, Jimmy Starace and his fiancé Tanya along with Tanya's Mom Nubia, there was our friend Ada from Napoli and Grace from Malta. We gathered around a table in Caffe Dante, drinking our espresso, Cappucino, and Caffé Maciato. The weather outside was great, about 48 degrees, with nice blue skies, puffy clouds, and clean crispy air. "Ah, Autum in New York, there's nothing like it." We were lucky as the forecast was origainally for rain, and here we were with about as good as a day you could ever want for Thanksgiving Day, not too warm, not too cold, just right.

So off we were in Jimmy's Mini Cooper, on our way to Jimmy's parents house for a traditional Turkey with all the trimmings dinner. Yes we had a nice juicy Roast Turkey. Ann did a great job. She also made mashed potatoes, tasty bread stuffing, fresh cranberry sauce, and green beans, and carrots. Pretty good. Everything was tasty. We start off with a nice little appetizer plate of spinach pie that Nubia made, along with absolutely scrumptious stuffed mushrooms. We drank wine of course, mostly Chianti, we had a bottle of Beaujolais, and a couple bottles of Macari Merlot. All was good.

For dessert the feast continued, and I know for me, that's what put me over the top, as far as getting bloated is concerned. I had to have a piece of everything, how can you resist? I had a piece of Strawberry Rhubarb Pie, half a cannoli, and my favorite, pumpkin pie. We had coffee of course, along with a special treat I bought for the ladies, a bottle of "Block E" dessert wine from Macari Vineyards. "Yummy!"

Well it's not just for ladies, but the bottle is not that big, and the ladies especially love it, so there you are, mainly for the ladies.

"So how did the Turkey turn into a deer you ask?" Here's how it happened. Not literally of course, just the way we like to phrase it. Jimmy's brother-in-law and his brothers like to go hunting in the Catskill Mountains in Upstate New York. They had shot a couple of deer a few days before and had a good amount of deer-meat (Venison) on hand. They know that Jimmy has quite a bit of dinner parties, so they asked him if he wanted some Venison. Jimmy being the eager gourmand that he is, said "yes" of course.

Collin being the nice generous guy that he is, took a chance with the break in the action of dinner after we had the turkey while we were taking time before moving on to dessert and coffee, he ran home to get the venison. He brought it back a leg, all wrapped-up, packed in ice, inside a cardboard box. Jimmy asked me if I would mind butchering it for him back at his and Tanya's apartment after we got back to Manhattan later in the evening. He said we could hang out and drink wine and he was curious to know how I would prepare the meat at a later date. So we finish up our Thanksgiving dinner at the home of Mr. & Mrs. James Starace Sr., and a wonderful dinner it was, real Americana.

We drive back to Greenwich Village and get situated. I take the meat out of the wrappings. It's a beautiful hindquarter, perfectly beautiful and fresh.

So we crack open a bottle of "nice Chianti" (sans human liver. "Ha ha!"), we turn on Ali G and I go to town on the leg of venison. Jimmy is amazed. It's nothing for me, I'm a professionally trained chef, but it's a little magical to the laymen. I broke down the leg into its major parts, we drank Chianti, watched

160

Ali G, laughing our asses off. The guy is hilarious. He did a number on Andy Rooney. Jimmy wanted to know how I would cook the Venison. I gave him the options available and we agreed to cut up most of the meat to make a large stew, along with some meat that I would use to make a Venison Ragu in a few days.

*A few days passed. It's the Sunday after Thanks-*giving. I bop over to Jimmy's place around the block on Macdougal Street and climb the 5 grueling flights of stairs to the apartment. It's a lot of work climbing all those stairs. You huff and puff, tiring, it is a grueling climb, and you need to catch your breath when you get there, but as so many of our friends know, for the meals that eat there, it's well worth the climb. Today's meal will be a Ragu Venison with Paparadelle. I'm sort of known as The Ragu King, as I make some of the best ragus known to man. As a famous line of Walter Brennan in a Western back in the 60's when he stated that he was the fastest shot in the West, his line was, "No Brag, Just Fact." Well, with all the great ragus I have made over the years, my famous Bolognese and Duck Ragu, ones of Rabbit, Squab, Veal, Wild Boar, you name it, but never venison. This was my first one.

I minced some onions, one clove of garlic, soaked some dry porcini mushrooms, and sliced button mushrooms. I brown the meat in a little olive oil, then added some of the Chianti we were drinking. I let the wine reduce by half before adding chicken broth and some tomatoes. I turned the flame down low, through in a bay leaf, salt, pepper, and a cinnamon stick and let the thing slowly simmer for three hours. The end result was phenomenal.

It was absolutely sublime. On a 100 point scale, it was easily a 98, if not, than more, "No brag, just fact." Hey, I don't have to say anything; I can quote the words of Tanya and Jimmy, "It was orgasmic." Yes the Ragu was delicious, the result of some beautiful Venison, perfect seasoning and cooking technique. It was a joy to make and even more of a joy to eat, as any good meal with loved ones should be.

That my friends is what La Tavola is all about, friends and family (Loved-Ones), sitting around a table laden with tasty food, wine, eating and drinking, savoring the food, the wine, the company, that's "La Tavola"

FEAST of The 7 FISH

My Aunt Helen used to make the famous Italian Christmas Eve Dinner, "The Feast of 7 Fishes," The 7 Fish of the Seven Sacraments. I know she made it because I used to hear her talking about it when I was a little kid. Although I've shared many wonderful dinners with Aunt Helen, I never had the pleasure of having the famous Christmas Eve Dinner "La Vigilia" The Feast of Seven Fish with her. We always had Christmas Eve dinner with the immediate family. My mother would make an Antipasto of Salami, Provolone, Peppers, and Olives, followed by Baked Ziti and a Baked Ham studded with cloves and Pineapple rings.

The first time I ever had the mystical dinner was about 12 years ago with my cousin Joe, his family and my girlfriend Duyen. We had been talking about this famous Italian feast a few weeks previous, and were thinking of making it. Joe told me he wanted to have the Christmas Eve Meal of The Feast of The 7 Fishes, known in Italy as La Viglia (The Vigil) or "La Festa Dei Sette Pesci," which is also known in Italian-America as The Feast of The 7 Fish, that signify the Seven Sacraments. Now, how's all that for a mouthful?

This Dinner, *La Viglia* originated in Southern Italy, especially in and around the invirons of Napoli. The Feast of The 7 Fishes is a Southern Italian tradition that does not exist in the rest of Italy, it is of the South. La Viglia, or "The Feast of the Seven Fishes" as it is known to Italian–Americans commemorates the waiting (Vigil) of the Baby Jesus to be Born at Midnight and the Seven Fish represent the Seven Sacraments of the Roman Catholic Church. Some also believe that the Seven Fish might signfy the 7 Days of Creation, but most believe the 7 Fish pertain to the Seven Sacraments.

So Joe asked me if I wanted to make this festive and all important dinner. To perform the ceromony. He didn't need to ask twice. I had never made it before and was dying to do so. For a long time I had yearned to partake in this celebrated old Southern Italian Ritual, and this was my chance. Naturally I was excited, so was Joe. The anticipation of the Great Feast to come was of happy expectations and excitement.

And what for the menu? I know Aunt Helen made Bacala, Shrimp Areganata, Mussels, Baked Clams, Calamari, Octopus, and eel, all much Loved Southern Italian (especially Napoli and Sicily) Creatures of the Sea. We decided which fish we wanted and how to cook each one. Much thought and planning went into the menu and its execution. Joe wanted;

165

Langoustines, Lobster, and Bacala. Alexandra asked if I would make Stuffed Calamari. We also decided on Shrimp Cocktail, Baked Clams Areganata, and Cozze al Posolipo. The menu was set. Duyen helped me with the Calamari which we stuffed with Shrimp, parsley, breadcrumbs, and Peas. We braised the Calamari with tomato, White Wine, and herbs. If I must say so myself, they came out superbly. The Stuffed Calamari were a lot of work to make, but well worth the effort as they were a huge hit with all. The Macari boys, Joey, Edward, and Tommy, as well as sister Gabriella, Alex, Joe, Duyen, Jose and Sergio from Barcelona were all in attendance.

The Mussels Posilipo were cooked with garlic, white wine, parsley, and tomato. The sauce is great to dip your bread into. This dish was one of my mother's favorites backin the days when few Americans other than those of Italian origins ever ate these wonderful little bivalves. Now-a-days everybody does. As a young boy I remember my mother sending me to Bella Pizza in East Rutherford to get an order of them for her. She always gave me a few and I have Loved them ever since.

Joe helped me to cook the Langoustines. They are hard to find and I had to order a ten pound box from Silvano in order to get them. The best way to cook langoustines is to split them in half and sauté them on each side in olive oil with a little butter and garlic. We served the Langoustines the same way as Silvano does as we feel his recipe is the best and everybody loves them that way. The Langoustines are served with a salad of thinly shaved fennel and celery dressed in olive oil and lemon with some split cherry tomatoes. Absolutely delicious!!!

The Lobsters we prepared the best way possible, the New England way, steamed and served simply with drawn butter and lemon wedges. There's nothing better on Earth, well except for Sunday Sauce of course.

Well, that Christmas Eve Dinner The Feast of Seven Fishes was quite a wonderful experience. It was a huge success but quite a bit too much work and actually, too much food, everyone was kind of full already by the fifth fish. The following year we decided on incorporating the Seven Fish into three courses instead of seven separate ones as it's just too much, too much to eat and too much to cook, a lot of work, and who needs to work that hard on Christmas. It was a good decision. We still had 7 different fish, which is a must. Serving these 7 Fish in three courses was a good idea as it is much more manageable that way, both to cook and to eat.

On this Feast of The 7 Fish in "3 Courses" we decided to make the Stuffed Calamari, which I would not have chosen again because it was a lot of work, but it was Alex and Joe's favorite and they said that it was a must. This was our Antipasto Course. Alexandra and her mom helped me, so the amount of work was cut down and divided into three. A good thing.

The stuffed calamari took care of two of the seven the shrimp that were stuffed into the squid.

The second course (Primi) of Linguine Frutti de Mare consumed four of the Seven Fish required for the meal. It consisted of Mussels, Clams, Lobster, and Scallops cooked with garlic, oil, herbs, and just a touch of tomato.

The seventh and final fish was fresh Cod that I roasted and served with a sweet and sour onion sauce (Bacala Fresca Agro Dolce). Everybody went bananas for it especially cousin Joe who raved at each and every dish I put down. It's a pleasure cooking for Joe as his passion for eating and for the Italian American way of life, the food, the wine, the rituals. Joe truly Loves and savors the experience, so I always love to cook for him, Alexandra, their children, or just about anyone for who savors the experience so well. This goes the same for my cousin Anthony Bellino his wife Debbie and their three girls Chrissy, Danna, and Allison, along with all my close friends and family.

It makes cooking a joy rather than a chore. When cooking for family or friends, you give two of life's great gifts, a tasty Home-Cooked meal combined with a little bit of Love. Scratch that. "A whole lotta Love!"

CAFÉ LIFE

It was not too long ago when well over 90% of the population of The United States was without access to one of life's great pleasures, something that is practically an absolute necessity of living, same as the Telephone, Television, Computers, and the Automobile. These Things most Americans could not in any way live without. Would you really want to? What is it, this necessity to living a Normal Happy Life? You want to know? It is the Café and Café Life. The simple act of having a pleasant space equipped with tables and chairs for you to sit, relax, have a Coffee, an Espresso, Cappuccino, Café Latte.

The cafe is usually a calm quiet place. There may be soft background music that is conducive to a pleasant tranquil mood, such as they play at Caffe Reggio on Macdougal Street in New York's Greenwich Village. At Reggio, they play the most calmingly beautiful Classical Music to go along with the delightful old Bohemian Greenwich Village ambiance that includes a Renaissance Wooden Bench from a Medici Palace in Florence, along with a painting from the School of Caravaggio of the Great Roman Artist Caravaggio who painted the World's Greatest rendition of "Bacchus" The Roman God of

Wine, along with numerous other fine works of art. "Really Fine!"

Yes the wonderful Paintings and Priceless Antiques only add to Reggio's delightful Charms. And you can sit on the bench, a Bench from a Medici Palace no less. Truly "Amazing." Any other place would have it roped off, and you wouldn't blame them if they did, but not at Caffe Reggio in Greenwich Village, you can sit in a priceless 500 year old piece of Renaissance Furniture. Only in New York Boys and Girls." Caffe Reggio is New York's oldest caffe, one of the oldest in the country for that matter, and you can sip your Cappuccino in a Medici Bench, looking at a Painting connected to Caravaggio, listening to lovely music of the time. It's quite nice.

So, back to cafes in general. The café absolutely must serve excellent Coffee of all types; Espresso, Cappuccino, Latte, so-on-and-so-forth, and this does not include "Ridiculous Concoctions" like a Double Soy Latte or Caramelo Cappuccino. I'm talking about real European Coffee here: Italian, French, Spanish, or Viennese style. The café should also have some type of sweet baked goods and maybe a few soups, salads, and sandwiches for people who need something Savory. All these things are required, along with interesting décor that conveys a warm, relaxed, casual feeling conducive to Hanging

Out, relaxing with or without friends, reading, writing, working, maybe meeting of business.

About twenty-one years ago I wrote a piece on the sad fact that except for a very few spots like New York, Boston, New Orleans, San Francisco and a few other blessed places in America, there were virtually no cafés in America. Very few anyway. There were far too few, and way to far in-between. The citizens of this great country had been largely denied, and for far too long. This was a "Wrong that Needed Righting." Something that was so vital to everyday living, part of the everyday life in the whole of Europe for a couple hundred years, this everyday necessity was missing from the lives of more than 95% of U.S. citizenry. "A true crime if there ever was one!" Even in a city as sophisticated and "Worldly" as New York, there were only a handful of cafes, and these were only in small pockets around town, like; Little Italy, The East Village, and Greenwich Village as well. The people in these neighborhoods were the fortunate few. If you lived in a neighborhood other than these, then you had the sad misfortune to be "Caféless," just like most of the other unfortunate souls in The United States of America. To me, and many others, this is was quite an unacceptable way to live. Especially if you're living in such a culturally cosmopolitan city as New York. Fortunately for me,

I have resided in neighborhoods that have a number of excellent café's within their borders, thereby affording me easy access within a few blocks of that very basic necessity to living a Normal Happy Life, a life "With" cafes, "The Café Life." Yes, I have been lucky enough not to have lived in a World without cafés. That is what most Americans went through before the only very recent café and Coffee-House boom in America. They lived in a "World Without Cafes." Sad! "Don't you think?"

By the way. The two neighborhoods I've lived in that I speak of naturally are Greenwich Village and before that, its counterpart, The East Village of New York City.

The functions that cafés provide in Europe are that they give people a nice place to go to accomplish two primary objectives. They go to either be with friends, spending time conversingon an infinite variety of subjects while enjoying each other com-pany over Coffee or Tea, and perhaps a Pastry or two.

They talk about Love, relationships, sports, politics, Art, Literature, the latest movie, the latest scandal, and Life in general. They bond. They live, in a life with Cafes.

The other big reason a person will go to a café is t o be alone to read, write, work, or to simply get away from the everyday hustle and bustle of life.

They go to relax, sitting at a quiet corner or window table, just watching the "World Go By," a famous Pastime of Cafes. Myself I do all these things and more. I am able to get all my reading and writing done in cafes. The café is peaceful and calm, and there are far too many distractions in my home to get any work done. I just put my head in a book and get lost, or else a little more productive, when I Put-Pen- to-Paper (now Fingers to Keypad). Sometimes I go to the café just because I want to get out of my apartment. When you live in a small dwelling as people do in New York, you need a little escape. Cafes are the perfect spot.

I go to cafes to spend time with friends, to chat and catch up on things. Working in the restaurant business for so many years, and working both lunch and dinner some days, I would have to get out of the place for an hour or two. There is no better place to relax and wind down, than at the nearest café.

For years, in Europe, the neighborhood café has been considered as a second home. Many people living in small apartments in Paris or other cities and especially New York would use cafes and restaurants as places to socialize and entertain if their apartments are too small to do so.

Cafes are great spots to rendezvous. I often do this with my girlfriend. You might be going to a museum, attending a concert, or going to a movie and need a spot to meet. Quite often a café is the best place to do so. Two happy cafe rendezvous' that are particularly memorable to me were, the time when my girlfriend Merceditas and I were in Paris and met my friend John Lee at Café Flore on Boulevard St. Germain in Paris before going to dinner at a nearby bistro.

Another great café rendezvous for me was the time I was inVenice and had to meet up with Jimmy Starace at Florian's in the Piazza San Marco. How's that for impressive rendezvousing? Cafes provide affordable food, drink, and shelter for you to get out of the cold for a hot drink, and to warm your cold bones. You can use a café as a library, a living room, office, or best of all, for "Romantic Interlude."

The café provides vital services to all and are necessary to living a proper life. After many years of being practically Caféless, America now has many. Actually, it all started about a year after I wrote my essay on the fact that the U.S. was almost completely Caféless. Though I am one of many who doesn't like Starbucks very much, most people love it. I have access to café's that are far superior, but it is thanks to this corporate giant that most Americans now have a nearby café available and are able to finally experience the wonders of café life. I guess, even if it is only Starbucks, that is better than not having any café at all. Well most Americans don't call Starbucks a café, they just call them Starbucks, never-the-less the type of business that Starbucks is, is a café, or call it a Coffee House.

So let's go from the cookie-cutter and the bottom of the barrel in Starbucks and talk about some of the World's great cafes. Caffe Florian situated in Piazza San Marco in Venice is one the World's oldest and most beautiful. Since 1720 this caffé has served the likes of Antonio Vivaldi, Casanova, Napoleon Bonaparte, Katerine Hephurn, Felini, and countless other celebrities, Princes, and Princesses, Kings, Queens, and heads of state.

There's Café Duex Maggot in Paris, which was a favorite of Hemingway, Sartre, and Simone de Beauvoir. Next door to Duex Maggot is Café Flore which was the favorite of Pablo Picasso. They are both great cafes, perfectly situated in the heart of St. Germain du Pre on the Left Bank. They have been serving Parisians and tourists for years. Just be sure to bring enough money to pay for a Six Euro (about $8.00) Café Latte. But it's worth it, just to be hanging-out at the same wonderful spots of some famous old writers and artists like Hemingway, Picasso, and Matisse. It's a small, affordable luxury to be sure.

In New Orleans, Café du Monde should be included amongst the World's Great Cafes. It is the absolute center of activity in "The Crescent City," where throngs of people flock for their famous Beignets and Café Crème. It's lots of fun and the "Big Easy's" best spot to people watch. Café du Monde is one of those rare places in the World where everybody just has to go to when in town. And this goes for both tourists and locals alike. You can't take a trip to New Orleans and not make at least one stop for beignets at Café du Monde. It just wouldn't be right.

I once went to a wonderful café that catered to the Portuguese colonials in Macau. The name of it is La Caravelle. I had been eating lunch outside at a nice little Chinese restaurant that was next to this Café. As I ate my lunch outside at the Chinese Restaurant I observed the expatriate Portuguese coming and going, greeting each other with a Kiss-Kiss on each cheek. It was a little piece of Portugal in a fara-way land for those Portuguese Expats. Watching the café, the comings and going of people, the activity in-side, I could see the place was special, so I naturally took myself there for my coffee and dessert. I had an Espresso, glass of water, and being in a Portuguese Café I naturally had to have a Pastelle, those tasty little Portuguese pastries of little Tartlets filled with Vanilla Egg Custard. I have Loved these things ever since long ago when my girlfriend Alexis and I were up in

Provincetown. Walking around we spotted a nice little Portuguese Bakery. We went inside, and this is where and when I first discovered those Portuguese Delights. Yumm! I was hooked for life, all the way to eating them at a Bakery–Café in Rio de Janiero more than twenty years later.

Way down in Buenos Aires, Argentina there is a the celebrated café that most Portenos go to, the grand Café Biela where my cousin Joe and I would sit outside under the magnificent "200 year old Rubber Tree' each and every morning we were in BA on route to our Argentine Wine Trip to Mendoza. Every morning we'd head over to Biela for breakfast of Café con Leche with great homemade Croissants. This is how we started off each day in the "Paris of South America," as they say. We had a great time down there in one of the World's Coolest of cities, Buenos Aires where we ate Tons of Grilled Meat, Tangoed, and started off each morning in Ricoletta with a Coffee and Croissants at the Café Biela.

Yes there are many wonderful cafes the World over. These are but a few. Go to them, enjoy them, live life in them, "Café Life."

CAFFÉ DANTE

Caffe'Dante, my home away from home, since 1985, I have probably been in there at least eight days out of every ten. If I can't make it for three days or so because of work or some other reason, I practically start having withdrawals. I'm not kidding. Mentally, it does something to me. I Miss it. Caffe Dante is located on McDougal Street in Greenwich Village. The doors were opened in 1915 and they've been going strong ever since. The caffé is owned by Mr. Mario Flotta, a gentleman from Avellino, Italy, just East of Naples by about forty-five minutes. Mario is very passionate about his caffe and the coffee he serves there. The best Cappuccino and Espresso this side of Rome. Espresso pulled just the right way and the perfectly balanced Cappuccino made from perfectly roasted beans from Italy, that Mario imports himself. The best money can buy. Mario wouldn't have it any other way.

The right way, is the only way for Mario at his celebrated caffe. It's great fun going there and chatting with him about all sorts of things like; food, Coffee, Italy, the restaurant business, and life in general, and about some of the "Old Characters,"

179

of Greenwich Village, like "Vinny the Chin" and "Jimmy Lollipops." Guys with Bent Noses and big bad Pinky Rings, if you know what I mean.

It's Mario's passion and dedication to operating an authentic Italian Caffe, which makes Caffe Dante the most fantastic caffe in all New York.

Besides the coffee, Mario, and the décor, the other great attraction, if not *thee* attraction, are the waitresses, especially Ada and Rose as well as the multitude of girls who have worked there over the years.

The décor helps to give the feeling of actually being in Italy, as it is exceedingly genuine, particularly the old coffee machine combined with the enormous Sepia pictures of Firenze, Dante Alighieri, my beloved Piazza Umberto in Capri, and other places in Italy.

It's nice to just sit there sipping your Espresso observing the goings on of this most special place, watching all the activity; the girls running around, serving the many regulars as well as students from NYU, with visitors from every corner of the Globe. Soft music plays in the background, as it should in any café. You hear the chatter of people conversing, the coffee grinder grinds freshly roasted beans, the Italian coffee machines hiss and huss steam as they spew that marvelous, ethereal brew of Italian Roasted Coffee Beans of Espresso. The end result is utter

180

perfection, a perfect Espresso. Listen to the clitter clatter of ceramic cups and saucers on the counter and tables. You will hear quite a bit of Italian spoken here as well as every other language under the Sun, as people of all nations pass through the Caffe doors.

If you like to read or write, you're in the right place. You can accomplish both as I have done over the years, reading a countless number of books, magazines, and newspapers, writing all sorts of essays, stories, articles, and this very book.

Claim your favorite table, order a steamy Cappuccino, sit back, relax, lose yourself in some Shakespeare, Machiavelli, Alighieri, Hemingway, Mark Twain, whatever. They'll all read better here, as they would at Café Flore, Duex Maggots, Biela, or Florian's on the Piazza San Marco, Venice. Yes Caffe Dante is every bit the equal of these famed Cafes of the World.

In weeks filled with long hours of hard work and all sorts of stress and aggravation, there are not many more pleasant things to do than to rest my tired bones and unwind, "Relax." It's like a Mind Body Massage, both. Yes, spending time in Caffe Dante will relax and rejuvenate you. This is what a great café can do, and Caffe Dante does it to perfection. And if, you're Lucky, you'll get to Chat with Mario. "I do all the time."

PROSCIUTTOLESS in NEBRASKA

It's a well-known fact that there have been tens of thousands of displaced Italian-American New Yorkers (Philladelphians, Bostonians and others too) over the years. Former Italian-American New Yorkers who have, for whatever reason, moved out of New York and relocated elsewhere. These people have been in serious distress, and mental anguish in their new Home-Towns pervades, as they quickly discover the the sad fact of the serious lack of good Italian Restaurants, Bakeries, Pork Stores and availability of quality Italian Food Products they need to live a typical Italian-American life. One that requires such things as a good Pizzeria, and Italian Specialty Shops stocked with essentials such as Prosciutto de Parma, good olive oil, fresh made Italian Sausages both sweet and hot, Parmigi-ano Reggiano, Cannoli, Espresso Beans and what not.

Yes there's a serious lack in most of this great country other than cities like Boston, Philly, New Orleans, and San Francisco. Other than these, citys, you're going to have a very hard time trying to find good Italian Restaurants, Pizza, and other items That are vital to living a normal, happy Italian-American life. "Not too much to ask for, wouldn't you say? But no!

It's a "Sad Hard Fact-of-Life" that many cities and towns in the U.S. are completely "*devoid*" of good Italian Restaurants, Pork Stores, good Pizzerias, a properly pulled Espresso, or specialty shops where people of Italian origins, who are in need of fresh Italian Sausages, Bread, Prosciutto, Salami, Parmigiano Reggiano, olive oil, fresh Mozzarella, Cannoli, and other products required to make pro-per Italian meals. These are simple necessities required to live a joyful productive life, being able to purchase good quality Italian food products, or going out to eat at a true Italian Restaurant, or Pizzeria. It's not too much to ask for. But "No," you're not gonna get what you need. Not in Nebraska, nor Iowa, or Boise too. There's just "No Prosciutto."

"Yes, believe it or not," there are many places in this great nation of ours, in this day and age, where the local citizenry are denied some of life's greatest treats, fresh made Mozzarella, real Italian Sausage, good Italian Restaurants, and properly made Pizza (Dominos, Papa John's and Pizza Hut, just ain't gonna cut it for an Italian-American). It may be alright for the local natives who were born in these deprived areas, but as for Italian-Americans who have moved to Culinary-Deficient areas, for whatever reasons, the deprivation caused by the lack of good honest Italian Food is enough to cause unnecessary anguish, yearning, and outright sadness.

Those of us who live in New York are extremely fortunate to have a plethora of these simple pleasures of outstanding Italian Restaurants, Pizzerias, Italian Pasrty Shops, Caffe's, Pasta Shops, Pork Stores, Wine Shops, and Italian Specialty Shops that supply us with every Italian culinary treat under the Sun.

Yes we are blessed with restaurants like Rao's, Gino's, Patsy's, Elio's, Rocco's, Bar Pitti, Frankie's Spuntino, Villa Mosconi's and others that serve tasty authentically prepared Italian food, along with bakeries that bake magnificent bread, Biscotti, Cheesecake, Cannoli, and other pastries. We have the best Pizzerias outside of Italy, like; Totonno's, Lombardi's, and John's of Bleecker Street.

In New York we have great Pork Stores that prepare wonderful fresh Italian Sausages, Braciola, Soppressata, Cacatitorini, fresh Mozzarella, and more. There are countless Italian food emporiums where you can buy imported Olive Oils, vinegar, pasta, Prosciutto de Parma, Mortadella from Bologna, Gorgonzola, Fontina, Aceto Baslamico from Modena, Porcini Secco, and the sinful Tartuffo Bianco of Alba in Peimonte (The Foot of the Mountain). The same place where astounding Barolos and Barbaresco wines come from. When White Truffles are in

184

season, from mid October through early January, this is thee sweetest time of he year for gourmands and food mavens everywhere.

We New Yorkers are blessed with amazing Italian Caffes, that serve authentic pastries, Gelato, and properly made Espresso and Cappuccino. We have Pork Stores and Delis, that sell fresh Italian Pork Sausages, Imported Italian Cheese, Salami, Olive Oil, Pasta, Prosciutto, and more. And we have butchers who know how to cut a "Proper Veal Scallopine and make Braciola ready for cooking. We have restaurants and Trattorias that know how to make authentic Bologn-ese Sauce, Spaghetti Carbonara, and Linguine Vongole. Culinarily, we want for nothing!

"My condolences to those Americans deprived of these simple little Pleasures. Excuse me, "Necessities" to good, Happy Living!"

SINATRA

Sinatra. The name? What does it that word, that name invoke? Well for me and millions of Italian-Americans over the years, the name Sinatra conjures mostly love, happiness, good-times, and "Pride." These emotions that are all one really need to be happy and content. That's what is important. Along with good health and family togetherness. And, by the way, you don't have to be Italian-American to love Sinatra, everybody does.

My love of Frank Sinatra, the man and his music began when I was a young boy growing up in East Rutherford, New Jersey, always in sight of the wonderous skyline of New York City. As far back as I can remember, my mother used to play all her fine records on her RCA Victor Record Player. Songs like Strangers in The Night, The Summer Wind, The Lady is a Tramp, Fly Me to the Moon, Come Fly with Me, and so many more. She played Sinatra all the time, along with Sammy, Dino, Elvis, Al Martino, Tony Bennett and Nat King Cole. Those were her favorites and Frank Sinatra was always number one for the entire Bellino Family, especially for Me, my Mother, Sister Barbara, and Uncle Frank.

The man sang with so much emotion that you could actually feel it within yourself, the feelings and emotions he was trying to convey. He tried and he always succeeded, whether he was singing a fun happy song like "Luck Be a Lady," "I've Got the World on a String", or the incredible way he sang a torch song, and sang these songs in a way no other could. Songs of lost love and Bittersweet Romances like "You and Me," The World We Knew, The Second Time Around, and "If I Had You," many others of course. You could feel the pain. They say the reason he had this very special touch with torch songs was because he was thinking of, and singing about the Greatest Love of his life, Ava Gardner, Frank's proverbial Girl That Got Away.

The man had such a way with lyrics and music, he'd take those songs and make them his own. These songs were, still are, and always will be wonderful gifts to his hundreds of millions of fans, to The World, to the history of mankind, to the Millions Who Loved and Adored Him.

We Italian-Americans are deeply proud that he was one of our own. He was an Icon, The Twentieth Century's greatest entertainer, a National Treasure and source of pride, whom Italians looked-up-to and could brag about, he was of Italian blood, same as us. That our roots were from the same place (my family in particular as the Sinatra Family came from the same Sicilian town as our Bellino Family is from, Lercara Friddi, Sicily) as well as so many of our forbearers of Italy to precede us, people like Leonardo Da Vinci, Bruneleschi, Giotto, Verrazzano, Columbus, Marconi, and Michael Angelo. There was Joe Di Maggio, Dean Martin, Tony Bennett, Al Pacino, Francis Ford Copola, Robert Mondavi, Jake La Motta, Rocky Marciano, and so many more, and of all those incredible people, Sinatra was tops. He still is.

There are have been all kinds of great singers in this World, people like Marvin Gaye, Diana Ross, Dean Martin, Michael Jackson, Al Green, Pavarotti, and on-and-on, but never a performer quite like Sinatra. His singing, the way he handled a song, was beyond compare. Frank sang with incrediable feelings and emotions.

If you were fortunate to ever see Sinatra perform perform live, it was an experience like no other. You know how he makes you feel so good when you listen to one of his many great recordings? Well multiply that by 100 and you just start to understand. The emotions one felt at a Sinatra Concert. Emotions quite similar to the magical euphoric feelings you'd get as a child running down to the Christmas Tree, opening your presents on Christmas Day. You'd get that special toy you'd been dreaming of, and. You are in Seventh Heaven. Euphoria! Do you remember?

For any great Sinatra fan, seeing the man perform live, being at a Sinatra Concert, it's akin to being a child again, under that Christmas Tree, to open that special present. That's a Sinatra Concert. Better!

When you went to a Sinatra Concert there would be so much love, joy, happiness, and adulation for the man that you could literally feel it in the air. It made you shiver and sent chills up and down your spine, "Literally." People would be screaming out, "We love you Frank", both men and women, and he'd reply back, "I love you too", in a way, only Frank could do. He truly did Love and appreciate his fans and had such a fantastic rapport with his audience.

Frank had great conversations with his audience. Guys felt as his pal, and women his lover, these are messages he conveyed, and his fans adored him for it. There have been so many great performers over the years, but there never was, there is not now, and there will never ever be another quite like that man, Francis Albert Sinatra. Never.

I've been a tremendous fan of his since early childhood. I grew up listening to the Beatles, Elvis, The Rolling Stones, all the great Motown and Philadelphia Sound artists, as well as many other Rock and Pop Stars.

Along with the Pop, R&B, and Rock music that most kids of my age would listen to at the time, I added artists of my parent's generation as well, artist like; like Sinatra, the rest of the Rat Pack, Louis Armstrong, Bobby Darin, and others. These artists that most children and young adults didn't listen to unless they were the chosen few who had the good taste and capacity to appreciate at tender young ages, musicians like; Armstrong, Sinatra, Ella Fitzgerald and others. No matter that these older artists were of their generation or not.

Sammy, Sinatra, Dean and others were great performers who made great music, and that all there was to it.

When I was in high school, I had a few friends who were heavily into Sinatra as well. Most kids thought he was boring and old-fashioned. We knew better! We were all of Italian ancestry and we were proud of him and of ourselves that although we were from another era, we were sophisticated enough, at such young ages to appreciate great performers of our parents and grandparents generation.We were Cool and we knew it! We looked at ourselves as The Jr. Rat Pack, Cool, Sophisticated, Confident!!! Frank gave us that confidence and bravado.

The sad day in which Frank Sinatra passed away, I received four messages of condolence, one from my sister Barbara, one from my brother-in-law Noel, one from my friend Selena, and one from my good buddy Jimmy Starace. That's how much I loved the man, and all my friends and family knew it, thus the messages of condolence. I wouldn't be surprised if that happened to a couple Million other Sinatra fans as well.

We were blessed with his presence for a long time. We still are, through all his fabulous recordings (12 Hundred Songs) and the memories, they evoke feelings of girlfriends, Love, our mothers, fathers, and of Frank.

I made sure that I went to see the man perform live on seven extraordinary occasions. These concerts hold many wonderful memories that I will have for the rest of my life, along with the numerous dinners with friends and family spent listening to his incomparable recordings and having Sinatra Parties on Saturday nights when WNEW AM in New York used to have a show every Saturday night for years called "Saturday with Sinatra", well, as only New Yorkers could do.

New Yorkers being Franks most loyal fans. This is where he got his start. The show was hosted by Sid Marx's. Sid and some of his special guests would tell all sorts of wonderful stories about Frank. There would be guests who knew Frank personally, as well as listeners who would call in and tell stories of how they "Fell in Love" listening to Sinatra or how they met him one time, or of performances that they went to. The show was three hours of listening to Sinatra's unrivaled music and of stories and antidotes of "The Man." For Sinarta Fans, this weekly Saturday Night Show was pure bliss.

Sinatra was loved all over the World, and people could tell you all sorts of interesting antidotes pertaining to all parts of the globe. I have a particular interesting memory of him combined with a great food and wine trip in Italy. I was in the small wine town of Greve in Chianti Classico, Italy having a nice little dinner with a friend. We were in this great little Enoteca eating the famed local Salumi and Paparadelle with Wild Boar Ragu. We were a bit surprised (I don't know why) to hear both Sinatra and Billy Holiday recordings playing at this little place. The owner walked by to see how we were doing. I gave him a thumbs-up and told him, "Great music".

"You like Billy Holiday?" he enquired. We had a nice little conversation with him about Billy, Sinatra, and wine.

He told us that he had lived and worked for a few years in New York. This guy was a big fan of Frank, Billy Holliday, and New York City. So, that's Sinatra, loved the World over, even in little towns like Greve in Chianti.

STEAK NIGHT

Our McDougal Street group of friends has in the past few years cultivated quite a nice array of rituals and traditions that we adhere to. Rituals that have enriched all our lives, rituals such as our regular dinner parties which have never had any specific name or theme to them. Well yes a theme in that they are All pretty much Italian Meals (99%) and we always play lots of great music. It's just that they were never labeled anything more than dinner parties, so we have these, then we started Mojito Mondays, and now the latest one that I'm about to tell you about.

So, the main theme though is that we share times at the table, this is always behind our regular dinner parties, Mojito Mondays or other. That's what it's all about, spending time at the table with friends and family, eating, drinking wine, and chatting as we listen to great music (No Rap, Techno, or Metal are allowed, "Never!").

These get-togethers bring great joy to all of us, making living in a city as fast paced and sometimes un-homey as New York, that much more pleasant and livable, giving us all a better sense of family and togetherness. We all have own particular circles of friends. For some reason or another some of our

closest friends have never, or rarely been to any of our meals and gatherings. Such has been the case
of one of my oldest and dearest friends, Mr. Raoul
Marti. Raoul has been to a few of our gatherings,
but not nearly as much as we'd like him to be, and
for the fact of being one of my closest and long
term friend. He's a great pal who's always there no
matter what. We all love him, Jimmy, Tanya, and
I, so when Jimmy ran into him a few weeks ago
they talked about getting together for dinner one
night. Jimmy said, "Let's do it!"

Raoul says, "Let's get Danny to cook, that Boy
can Cook his Ass off. I'll buy the Steaks and we'll
let Danny cook."

So it was set. We decided on the following Monday
night, and Steak Night was on its way.

We went to   Ottomanelli's and picked up some
fine Prime Aged Sirloin Steaks, New York Cut, 2
inches thick. I picked up some potatoes and some
good old Iceberg Lettuce and cucumbers for salad
which we had as a starter with fresh roast red
peppers dressed in olive oil and one of Mr. Marti's
favorites, Assiago Cheese.

I started the sautéed potatoes first, just the way
Raoul likes them, ever since we had them for lunch
one day when we were in Paris with one of Raoul's
ex-girlfriends who was in Paris with some other
friends working in the fashion industry during the

Paris Spring Prete de Porte Shows. The girls were all working during the day, so Raoul and I went to a great little Bistro that our friend John Lee recommended to me a few years back, "La Palette" on Rue d' Seine in Saint Germain de Pres. It's a great little Bistro. We walked in there one day, and the place was packed. The owner, Jean Marie, has a reputation for be a little bit of a Hard-Ass. If he doesn't like you, simply because he doesn't like you, it's not good. So I was a bit worried as to whether we'd meet Jean Marie's approval or not. We walked in and he greeted us and telling us to wait at the bar and he'd have a table for us in a few minutes. "So-far-so-good."

La Palette is a real neighborhood place. Not a tourist in sight. Other than us that is, but hey, we're not tourist, we're Hip New Yorkers. Ha-Ha!

It was lunchtime and the restaurant was full of businessmen, secretaries, hop girls, and elderly neighborhood l adies lunching solo or with a friend. The place was full of energy. It had a great Vibe and we were excited, and eager for a nice lunch.

La Palette is your quintessential Parisian Bistro. It has a warm delightful feeling, as any good bistro should. It's furnishing and décor fit the part. You know what I mean? The food is simple, delicious,and affordable. The waiters are dressed in the traditional Parisian Bistro Waiters Garb of; black

195

pants with white shirts, Black Vest (pockets filled with Pens and Corkscrew) Black Bowties, and long flowing white aprons, as is the proprietor Jean Marie, he dresses just like the waiters who work for him.

So we sit down and look at the menu. I'm excited to see that they are serving one of my favorites that day, Pomme Daphinoise. I explain what they are to Raoul and he's hopped-up to try them as well. We both order a couple steaks with Pomme Dauphinoise and when Raoul orders a ham and cheese sandwich as an appetizer Jean Marie looks at him sort of funny, but doesn't say anything. He tells us that they have run out of Pomme Daupinoise, but they have Pomme Saute. We settle for them instead. Lunch was great! Our Steaks and the sautéed Potatoes were wonderful.

One of the best Steak Dinners of ever had. Superb! When we finished eating, Raoul asked Jean Marie if we could smoke the Cuban Cigars that we had bought.

"But of course," beamed Jean Marie. We ordered a couple Cognacs, sparked-up the Cuban Cigars, and we were in Seventh Heaven; in Paris, at a great bistro, with tasty food, a cool vibe, and finishing up with some fine Cognac and a couple of Cuban Cohibas, and being accepted by Jean Marie. Now this was one fine day.

We had a great time and were accepted by Jean Marie, so when it was time for lunch the next day and I asked Mr. Marti where he wanted to go for lunch, Raoul was quick to reply, "let's go to La Palette."

I said suprisingly, "You want to eat there again?" "Why not? It was great," Raoul retorted. And indeed it was. Raoul is smart enough to know that you stick with a winner, and La Palette is just that. When we walked into La Palette again that day, and it was packed as usual, Jean Marie beamed and said, "Hello my friends, I'll have a table for you in a few minutes." It's good to feel accepted and wanted. Jean Marie gave us the same great corner table we had the day before. So Raoul and I sat down for another memorable meal, a lunch at La Paltette on the Rue de Seine in the Great City of Light, Paris, France, Voila! "We had it made in the shade. Made in La Palette that is," and all was fine in the World. Well, Paris anyway!

See how you can bring up one subject and go on a tangent about it? I was talking about Steak Night and go off about Paris and La Palette. "Hey it's a great little story, that is pertinent to this one about Steak Night."

So, let's get back to our latest, greatest new tradition, "Steak Night." It's pretty simple and straight forward after I spent the time on Pomme Saute (sautéed potatoes). Here's how it goes. We picked up some great Steaks from Ottomanelli's.

I make tasty sautéed potatoes, just the way my buddy Raoul likes them, as do I, Jimmy, and Tanya as well. Let us not forget my cousin Tony Bellino who once asked me, "How the Hell do you make the potatoes taste so good?"

"Top Secret Tony."

Tony was once a little hurt and deflated one time when he asked his wife Debbie who is real Steak Lovers if she wanted him to cook a steak for her one night? Debbie said, "No thanks. Danny is coming over tomorrow, I'll let him cook one." Meaning, not that she doesn't want Tony to go through all the trouble, but that she likes the way I cook a steak better than her husband Tony.

"Sorry Tony, but Facts are Facts"

Just kidding. In all fairness to my cousin Tony, he is actually an excellent cook. Of course he is. His mother, Fran Bellino was one of this country's great Italian American Home-Cooks, and Tony's Dad and Fran's husband, Uncle Tony is as we've already mentioned, quite the good cook as well. But when it comes to Steaks, I cook one of the best, better than some famed Steak Houses. "No brag, just fact," and I've proven it many times over.

So there was a new tradition we started. We call it "Steak Night." The participants will usually be myself and Raoul, Jimmy and Tanya will always be there, and we'll invite one or two other guests, as well as any ladyfriends any of us happen to be seeing at the time sometimes.

We get together with this close knit group of friends, cook up some tasty Steaks, Potatoes, a Salad, and maybe some roast peppers and cheese. We listen to some good music, drink wine, relax, and chat about this and that, and we have the best time imaginable. It's what we do, great times with friends and family, around the table, "La Tavola."

The NEGRONI

The Negroni! A cocktail most Americans do not know. Too bad! With its contents of bitter Campari, Sweet Vermouth, and Gin, the Negroni is quite the unique cocktail. Best of all, it's tasty and refreshing, with the essence of an Orange Peel, it invigorates and rejuvinates. The Negroni is wonderful any time of the year, however, it is especially pleasing on a hot Summers day somewhere on the Coast in Italy, The South of France, or anywhere on the Mediterranean, or the Hamptons or South Beach for that matter.

So, not many people know of the Negroni and its charms, other than the more Sophisticated among our population. Even just a minute percentage of those who have traveled to its birthplace in Italy will even know of the cocktail. In this country, it is drunk more often in the city of New York. A city with a higher "Sophisticate" ratio than most, but even still, just a few will know of this drink, the Negroni Cocktail. You might find people drinking them in the great food & drink city of New Orleans, San Francisco by the bay, or Miami. In Idiana and the Mid–West? Not so much!

So what it is it? Well its base is the highly popular aperitif of bitter Campari, a Bitter–Sweet aperitif from Torino, Italy. The Negroni is made of 1 ½ Oz.

Campari, 1 ½ oz. Sweet Vermouth, 1 & 1/2 oz. Gin, over ice cubes in a Rocks Glass, and garnished with a slice of Orange or Orange peel. Voila!

The Negroni is usually drunk as an aperitif before dinner in the early evening, but just wonderful anytime of the afternoon, especially Alfresco, or late into the evening day. A Negroni is a particularly splendid drink for a leisurely Afternoon Cocktail or two. As a matter of fact, I just had a couple nice afternoon Negroni's at Cipriani Downtown just the other day.

The base of the Negroni Cocktail is the Italian bitter Aperitif Campari created in Novaro, Italy near Milano in the 1860 by Gaspare Campari. The secret recipe that has been carefully guarded for more than 150 years consists of and infusion of alcohol, Herbs, and vegetables, including, Orange Peel, Chinotto, and other secret ingredients.

The Negroni Cocktail was created in 1919 at the Caffe Casoni in Florence, Italy when the Count Negroni, a regular customer of the caffe, asked his waiter for a Americano that had a little more of a kick to it. The Barman and waiter obliged the Count with a cocktail made with the normal Campari, and Sweet Vermout of the Americano but with the addition of London Dry Gin. The Count Loved the Cocktail which was named after him and thus the Negroni was born.

"Do You Remember Your First Time," was the slogan of a wonderful Ad Campaign by Campari with pictures of good looking men or Gorgeous Women, and some sort of Campari Cocktail in hand, usually the most famous of Campari and Soda with a twist of Orange. The Ad was asking you if you remember the First Time you had your first Campari, but of course there was the Sexual connotation eluding to the first time you had Sex.

A ploy often used by marketers and ad agencies.
I remember "My First." It was of course on my first trip to Italy in 1985 sitting outside at a Caffe on The Piazza Popolo in Rome. I had seen the ads and people drinking them outside and when my waiter came over, I ordered one. It took a little getting used to at first, but I loved it and have ever since, and I've turned many people on to the drink ever since. On a whole, just a small percentage of Americans have ever even tasted Campari at all, whether it's a Campari and Soda, Campari & OJ, or my beloved Negroni.

If you've never had one, it's time to get on the stick.

We drink them like crazy at my buddy Pat Parrotta's house. Pat is an Italian Wine Lover, who throws great dinner parties, and he's quite the dam good cook. We eat Pasta, Chicken, Steaks,

Sausages, whatever, always with some nice Italian Wine.

So "Yes" Pat is a great host who knows how to throw a dam good dinner party. His dinners parties are always a huge success and we always start the day off with what has become a tradition at Pat and Gina's home, a couple tasty Negroni's or Campari Spritzers to get things rolling. I always look forward to having my Negroni when I get to Pat's after riding the Ferry over from Manhattan.

As I've already stated, Pat is a wonderful Host who has great enthusiasm to cook for friends and family, serving some nice Italian Wine, along with his celebrated Negroni's which are better than just about any Bartender in New York. "For Real!"

Making a good Negroni, brings to mind, that it's not that easy. Not everyone can do it, as you need to get the proper balance of these very prominent ingredients of Campari, Gin, and Sweet Vermouth. I can, and Pat can, but many a bartender does not, no matter what they may think. I've been extolling the "Wonders" and Virtues of Campari and the Negroni for well over 20 years, while just a few American's on a whole have yet to discover it.

Even as now some big cocktail association has named the Negroni, "The Cocktail of The Year" for 2011. People are just now catching up. I could have told you 20 years ago. In fact, "I did."

Anyway, back to thes bartenders who don't know how to make a proper Negroni. I was recently at a popular restaurant that has two bars inside where they make the new So-Called Artisanal Cocktails and House Specialty Drinks, made by "Mixologists?"

I ordered a Negroni. The Bartender made it and served it to me straight-up in a cocktail glass. I asked him to put it in a Rocks Glass with ice, whereby he gave me an almost disdainful look, as if he made a great drink the right way and who the Hell was I to have him alter it. "These Mixologist." Well, first off, the drink was not great. It wasn't even good. It was out of balance, and as I've said, in making a proper Negroni, it's all about balance. I know the balance, Pat knows the balance, that bartender did not. Not for a "Proper Negroni" any- way. I've been drinking these things for more than 20 years, and I'm not going to have some bartender "Who Just Fell Off the Turnip Truck" tell me how to drink my beloved Negroni. "Not gonna Happen!"

So my friends, if you've yet to imbibe in one. Don't you think it's hightime? Just make sure to get a bartender who knows the ropes. I suggest Cipriani Downtown.. Even better, the families flagship restaurant, Harry's Bar, Venice, a Bar, Caffe, or restaurant in Rome or on the Amalfi Coast.

ON ITALIAN WINE

Italy has a long illustrious history in wine dating back to the Roman Empire and the Ancient Greeks who planted some vineyards in Sicily and parts of Southern Italy. The Romans with their far reaching Empire that stretched across Europe and into North Africa, planted vineyards in every corner of their domain, including; France, Germany, Spain, and Croatia.

Wine is as deeply rooted into the Italian lifestyle as Pizza, Pasta, Prosciutto, and Parmigiano.

When it comes to wine there is no country on Earth that can compare to Italy. If you look at wine maps of other major wine producing countries, you will see that vineyards are planted in just a few areas here and there as far as the entire land mass is concerned. Italy on the other hand has vines planted in the whole of the country, from Friuli in the North-East down to the toe of Calabria in the South-West and everywhere in-between, along with the large islands of Sardinia and Sicily. No matter where you go in Italy you will find grape vines growing. There is no country in the world with such a multitude of grapes being cultivated, furthermore there is no country on the planet that has the diversity in wine styles and grape varieties grown.

The number of grape varieties in Italy is staggering as compared to other countries. In comparison, take the United States, France, and Australia for example, three of the top wine producing countries in the World. In terms of both quality and quantity.

In Australia and the U.S. the primary grapes produced are Chardonnay, Sauvignon Blanc, Merlot, Cabernet Sauvignon, Syrah, and Pinot Noir. Add to this a fair amount of Reisling and Gamay, a bit of Cabernet Franc, Pinot Bianco, Petit Verdot, and Petit Syrah and a few other varieties and you have the major grapes grown in these countries.

France cultivates these varieties and more, including Muscadet, Grenache, Viognier, and Carrignan. No doubt they have a nice variety of great wine produced in France. Wines that I love, especially from the Rhone, Bordeaux, and Loire Valley, but for all the wonderful wines from France they can't come close to touching Italy in number of styles and grape number of grape varieties found in Italy, not even close. So, for my money, Italy is thee Worlds Best!

There are a number of grape varieties that are grown in Italy and nowhere else or in such minuscule amounts that they are of no consequence.

One example, Nebbiolo, the solitary grape that makes up the famed Barolo and Barbaresco wines of Peimonte. Nebbiolo thrives mainly in Peimonte and in Lombardia next to Piemonte, but no place else in World, although it has been grown in small amounts in California and Virginia with mediocre results and in such minuscule amounts it is inconsequential.

As well as being the single grape variety that makes up the famed Barolos and Barbarescos, Nebbiolo is the grape of Gattinara, Nebbiolo d'Alba, and several other wines of Peimonte.

Wines made of Nebbiolo are Wine World Stars with producers like Angelo Gaja, Aldo Conterno, Giacomo Conterno, Bartolo Mascarello, Renato Ratti, and the great Bruno Giacosa, to name just a handful of famous producers who make legendary Barolo and Barbaresco wines.

A few other fine grape varieties that are grown in Italy and nowhere else are grapes like Ruche, Negroamaro, Nero d' Avola, Ciliegielo, Monduese, and Picolit.

Along with the indigenous varieties, Italy has great examples of the Big Four of the Wine World; Chardonnay, Cabernet Sauvignon, Merlot, and Syrah. With the tremendous amount of indigenous grape varieties along with the "Big Four" it makes for an infinite amount of styles that can be made of single varietal wines or an endless range of wines that are proprietary blends in which Italy makes by far the greatest number in the world. And I might add, many are unique to Italy alone, with infinite results and possibilities to all the indigenious native wines, there are examples of native Italian grapes being blended with the popular Big Four of Cabernet Sauvignon, Merlot, Chardonnay, and Syrah.

One example of how proprietary wines made in Italy, blending native Italian grapes with popular international grape varieties would be the renowned Super Tuscan wine "Solaia" which blends 75% Cabernet Sauvignon with 5% Cabernet Franc and 20% native Sangiovese. Another blending of popular international grapes being blended with Italian ones is one of thee greatest white wines in the World, the legendary "Cevaro della Salla" from Ummbria which blends 85% Chardonnay with 15% of the native Umbrian Grechetto. The grapes are Barrell Fermented and aged in French Oak and th end results is of a elegant White Burgundy of the highest caliber. These are just two of a multitude of celebrated examples of the different styles of Italian Wines.

For any wine drinker interested in exploring the endless variety of interesting wines, with a never ending realm of possibilities of taste and styles, they need look no further than Italy. It's the top of the ladder, but the sad fact is that for all of the hundreds of millions of people who drink wine regularly, there are just a small percentage who really delve into the great depths of all that is available. The large majority of wine drinkers keep drinking the same old things over and over, The Big Four, and if they do drink some Italian wines, most just drink Pinot Grigio, Chianti, Brunello, Amarone, Valpolicella, and little else. This great peninsula has so much to offer, it's mind boggling, wines like; Barbera, Vermentino, Salice Salentino, Taurasi, Tocia, Aglianico d'Vulture, Greco d' Tufo, Brachetto, Fiano d'Avelino, Ripasso, Friesa, and Nero d' Avola, just to name a very few.

The most famous and legendary wines of Italy are of the celebrated Barolos and Barbarescos, Vino Nobile, Brunello, Chianti, Amarone, and a multitude of famed Super Tuscans. What is a Super Tuscan? Many people will ask. It is mystifying to many, exactly what they are. It's a question that is a little hard to explain, but I will do just that.

First off, a Super Tuscan Wine is a wine made in Tuscany, where in specific DOC and DOCG zones of wines like Chianti, Brunello, Morellino de Scansano, and Vino Nobile are made. To be called Chianti, Brunello, or Vino Nobile, these wines must be made within the geographic boundaries of the specific DOC or DOCG Zone, and they must be made according to the laws set by the Italian government, pertaining to the type of grapes that can go into the particular wine, the amount of grapes that can be harvested per acre, prescribed amounts of time the wine must be aged in wood, and when the wine may be released for sale. Super Tuscans, are wines made in any of these particular zones in Tuscany, but are not made according to any government rules. A producer of any particular property can put whatever grapes he wants into the particular wine and give it whatever proprietary name he chooses.

There was a time period from the 1960's and into the 70's it is sad to say that Italy on a whole was producing a lot of really poor quality wine. They were going for quantity and not quality. This trend was spawned by the Italian government itself. In the case of Chianti for example, the laws to be followed for making this wine amounted to a recipe for making inferior wine. The governental laws allowed for high yields of grapes per acre (which is not good for making good quality wines) and allowed the addition of up to 30% of Trebbiano, or as low as 5% in the blend for Chianti. Chianti being a red wine and Trebbiano being a white grape, this was an insane concept. So it was up to each individual producer in the Chianti zone to make either smaller amounts of good quality wine or large amounts of bad wine.

You understand that you didn't have to put 30% white grapes in the blend if you didn't want to, butif you did want to, by law you could do it, and the wine still qualified as being Chianti, according to the laws.

In the early 1970's there were a few pioneers in Tuscany that were appalled by what was going on and decided to make great quality wines in the regions of Morellino in Bolgheri on the Tuscan coastline and in the Chianti Clasico zone. These wines would be of great quality, because they were made with Cabernet Sauvignon and Cabernet Franc. These wines would not qualify as any DOC or DOCG wine. So these new wines which were of the highest quality would by law have to be labeled as IGT or Vino d' Tavolo wines, which is the lowest of the classifications. In the end didn't really matter, because everybody who knew anything about wines knew that they were great.

So it was Mario Incisa Rocchetta who on the Tuscan coast in Bolgheri made the first of the now very famous Super Tuscan wines with his famed Super Tuscan Wine "Sassicaia," which is made with a blend of 85% Cabernet Sauvignon and 15% Cabernet Franc, aged in small French Oak Barrels, rather than the large Slovenian Oak ones that were the norm for hundreds of years in most of Italy.

His cousin Piero Antinori soon followed suit in the Chianti Classico zone with the equally famous Tignanello, usually made with about 15% Cabernet Sauvignon, 5% Cabernet Franc, and about 80%

Sangiovese aged in small barrique barrels as well. Though thin 1971, the first vintage Tignanello was made solely of Sangiovese and was labeled as Chianti.

Wine critics recognized the quality of these wines immediately, and it was the British wine writers and critics who started calling these great non-traditional wines of Tuscany, "Super Tuscans." The nickname caught on and it stuck to this day, although the name is unofficial and has never been recognized by the Law makers in Italy.

Oh, are you still confused? To break it down in simpler terms, a Super Tuscan can actually be made from any grape or blend of two or more. The wine is a proprietary wine that is made strictly according to the style that the Proprietor of a vineyard wants to make and is usually influenced by what grapes are growing on the particular property or what kind the owner may want to plant and add to the vineyard.

Super Tuscan wines can be anything. The most common examples are several, wines made with 100 percent Sangiovese as with "le Pergole Torte" from Montevertine, or Flacinella from Fontodi in the beautifully gorgeous town of Panzano in Chianti Classico. Super Tusan wines can be made of 100% Cabernet as is "Il Pareto" from Nozzole and Cinghiale. The eminent Masetto from the Ornellaia Estate of Ludvico Antinori is made from 100% Merlot, as is "L'Aparita" from Castello d'Alma.

"Tignanello" is normally made of about 85% Sangiovese, 10% Cabernet Sauvignon, with 5% Cabernet Franc while its Sister Wine "Solaia" is made of 75% Cabernet Sauvignon, 5% Cabernet Franc, and 20% Sangiovese.

So, Super Tuscans can be made from anything that a Proprietor wants to make his with, though the most popular grapes are Cabernet Sauvignon, Sangiovese, Merlot, Cabernet Franc, and Syrah, and with these grapes, a Super Tuscan can be made with 100% of just one grape, or a blend of two or more grapes. These are not the only grapes, however they are the most prevalent and 90% of all Super Tuscan Wines are made up of these Five Grapes. The main areas that Super Tuscan Wines come from are Bogheri, Chianti Classico, The Maremma, and Montalcino, thought they can come from any place in Tuscany.

Now, back to Chianti. So, now that the laws governing the make-up of Chianti have changed for the betterment of this storied Italian wine, the quality has tremendously improved. I do not however agree with the new laws allowing small percentages of Merlot, Cabernet Sauvignon, and other French Vinifera in the blend or the fact that Chianti can be made solely with Sangiovese. This practice is "Sacrilegious" and should be stopped. It's a Sin that the Italian Government allows for grapes like Cabernet and Merlot into the blend which take over and dominate Sangiovese, ruining the balance of one of Italy's most wonderful and thee number 1most Iconic of all Italian Wines. Chianti is of Chianti and Italy and should taste like Chianti, not like a Super Tuscan Wine which may or may not be made of international grape varieties, which is fine if you are making a Super Tuscan Wine and labeling it thus. But to add Merlot or Cabernet Sauvignon to a wine labeled Chianti, crushes it wonderfully rich heritage and taste of the Chianti Classico Region and of the Tuscan soil. Yes, "This is Sacrilege." Chianti should taste like the Tuscan soil it comes from, "Chianti should taste like Chianti, Not Bordeaux" or something other than Chianti."

In keeping with the great old tradition of Chianti, it should always be a blended wine dominated by mostly Sangiovese with a small amount of a local secondary grape or grapes like Cannaiolo, Colorino, Malvasia Nero, Cielegiolo, or Mammolo, all native varietal secondary blending grapes of the region. I would even add Trebbiano to the allowable grapes as long as they didn't exceed 2% of the blend. This is Real Chianti, "True Chiant." If someone wants to make a wine with some of the international varietals, "Fine." Just label the wine as a Super Tuscan and not as Chianti. Any wine made with any grapes other than Sangiovese and the previously mentioned minor native secondary grapes, it is not True

Traditional Chianti. A wine made with mostly Sangiovese and either Merlot or Cabernet Sauvignon in the Chianti Classico Region, "Is Not Chianti" and should not be called Chianti, and "Should Not Be Allowed to Label it Chianti." It is "Not" Chianti.

It is a "Super Tuscan" and should be labeled as such, and the European Union should get on the case of the Italian Government to change the Laws Governing Chianti once again. They should "Eliminate" the practice of allowing Merlot, Cabernet Sauvignon, and any other International Grapes that are not Native to the Chianti Classico Zone, and go back to the "Original Formula" set down by Barone Bettino Ricasoli in the 1860's, of Chianti to be made with a blend of primarily Sangioves Grapes and small percentages of secondary blending grapes of Canaiolo, Malvasia, and or other native grapes.

I must admit that Chianti, Brunello, and some of the Sangiovese based Super Tuscans are my favorite wines in the World, especially those of my good friends who make the most wonderful wines you could ever wish to drink. Wines like Prunaio (100% Sangiovese Grosso) and the Chiantis from Alessandro Landini, the proprietor of Fattoria Vitticio, Conti Sebastiano and Nicolo Capponi the aristocratic owners of the historical Villa Calcinaia in Greve. The Capponi produce great Chianti, Grappa, luscious olive oil, and one of the finest Vin Santo's I have ever tasted. This Vin Santo is perfectly balanced with just the right amount of acid and a weight that is not too clawing or viscus as some desert wines can be. The Villa Calcinaia Vin Santo is, I might say "Perfect."

Another good friend, Vittorio Fiore and sons Roberto and Jyuri make the renowned 100% Sangiovese Super Tuscan wine Il Carbonaionne at their vineyard Podere Scallette, high up on a hill in Greve that overlooks the entire Chianti Classico zone with Firenze in the north and Siena to the south. The vineyard commands one of the most spectacular views in all of Chianti Classico..

Also in Greve is the fine estate of Vignamaggio, where it is believed the World's most famous painting, the Mona Lisa was painted by Leonardo di Vinci, at Vignamaggio. Perfection still follows Da Vinci with the most superb wines imaginable, that includes; one of Italy's greatest single varietal Cabernet Franc, the Super Tuscan "Obsession." Also from Vignamaggio is the fabulous namesake wine "Mona Lisa," the estates Chianti Classico Riserva, it's "Fantastic." With a name and pedigree like that, it just has to be!

I am not saying that Chianti is the World's best wine. No, it is my personal favorite, lighter in body than Brunello and not as big as Amarone or some Super Tuscans, but for me, the perfect wine to drink with any of the Italian Food made by either myself, my Aunts, Uncles, cousins, or one of Italy's many wonderful cooks. The Sangiovese grape that makes up most of the Chianti blend and is in whole or part of many Super Tuscans as well as Vino Nobile and Brunello is absolutely my favorite, along with a few Million others around the World.

For anyone who like's Big Ass powerful full bodied wines, you'll not get it with Sangiovese. What you'll get is a wine that has a lot of flavor without being powerful, that is of the proper weight to complement food at its best, instead of overpowering and clashing with food as concentrated Cabs, Syrah, Merlots, and blends of California and Australia do. Chianti are the most perfect wines for most any of Italy's vast Regional Cuisne. It goes well with anything, whether, Pasta, Meat, Poultry, and even Fish.

There is some Enchanting Lure and History behind Chianti and the wine zone that it is produced in, which many feel is the "Most Beautiful Wine Region in the World," with its lovely rolling hills, filled with wondrous rows of Grape Vines, Olive Groves, Castles, Stone Farm Houses, and Cypress Trees that seem to dot the crest of almost every hill.

Other important indigenous wines of Tuscany are Vernaccia, Vino Nobile, Morellino, Carmignano, and the highly exalted Brunello di Montalcino, along with Amarone, Barolo, and Barbaresco, Italy's most esteemed native wines. Most of the great native wines of Tuscany are red. Tuscany is Red Wine country, and the only important native white is Vernaccia from the beautiful medieval hilltop town of towers, San Gimignano.

There is an old saying amongst many Italian men. If you ask them if they are white or red wine drinkers? They'll reply, "White wine? What is the point?" In other words. Why would you even think of drinking white wine when you have red which is so much better? To some point, I do agree with them as I drink red about 90% of the time, but there are many great wines in the World, and they offer a different wine drinking experience and have some flavors and characteristics such as certain mineral and floral qualities that you don't get in reds. White Wine should not be dismissed so easily. White Wine is good too. White's are not inferior to Red Wines, different animals, and they each have their own attributes. So if you mostly drink Red Wine, don't look down at people drinking whites. It's Ok. I was once guilty of this act. I've changed we all do. And as they say, "To each his own." Or is that Sausage his own?"

So, if you're having a nice long serious meal, it's great to start the meal with a glass of white to get your palate jump started before moving on to one or more reds. Variety is the spice of life.

The White Wines of Italy! Here again in my opinion, Italy makes the best, although I know many would disagree, and I'm likely to get some serious arguments, but I'll stick by my guns in affirming that Fruili Venenzia Giulia is the greatest white wine region in the World today. Many would say that White Burgundies are the best whites in the world and that Burgundy is the greatest white wine producing region. Well I would agree number one that White Burgundies are the World's best white wines, but although Burgundy produces the World's greatest whites, it is not the greatest white wine region, that honor goes to Friuli. The reason is quite simple.

Yes, White Burgundies are the single greatest white wines, but they are of just mainly of one grape variety, (with small amounts of Aligote and Sauvignon Blanc) Chardonnay. Friuli–Venezia Guilia on the other hand makes white wines of the highest quality as in Burgundy, but unlike Burgundy where the wines are mainly of one single grape variety, the great wines of Friuli are made with a much greater number and selection of various grape varieties. Varieties like Tocai, Sauvignon Blanc, Picolit, Reisling, Pinot Grigio, Pinot Bianco, Verduzza, Traminer, Chardonnay, Ribolla Gialla, and Muller

Thurgau which are all made in single varietals in different styles and in various micro-climates to create wines that express the both the varietal character of each grape and the geographical influences in a host of ways.Then there are the numerous proprietary blends like the prestigious wines of Sylvio Jermann who produces the famed Vintage Tunnina, Vinnaia, and Dreams, as well as the great wines of Schiopetto, Livio Felluga, Gianni Venica, and a host of others.

With all these different single varietal wines made in various styles and the endless possibilities of making proprietary blends, these are the factors that make Friuli-Venezia-Giulia the World's preeminent quality white wine making region in this World.

The wine making region of Friuli is to white wines, what Tuscany is to red wine, the greatest white wine producing region in the world, bar none! And these wines are now being coined "The Super Whites", the name fits.

White Burgundy? The wine is made of what? One-Hundred percent Chardonnay, a grape variety that has gained some disdain amongst many wine drinkers around the world. This is what happens when any grape or wine becomes overly popular.

This was the case with Soave in the 70's, Chardonnay in the 90's, and now Merlot. As some say, ABC. "Anything-But-Chardonnay!"

So, if you want to be adventurous and gain some unique wine knowledge that few others around you would have, delve into the marvelous array of the unique wines of Southern Italy and grape varieties like Piedrossa, Negroamaro, Nero d'Avola, Primitivo, Frapatto, Munduese, Nerello Mascallese, and Aglianico.

Aglianco, which is considered the greatest red varietal of the south, comes mainly from the regions of Campania and Basilicata, and are made in both single varietal wines, as well as Aglianico being blended with Merlot, Cabernet, and or other grapes. In Campania they grow other grapes you will not find outside of Italy, like Piedirosso, Coda di Volpe, and Fiano, of which is made one of Italy's premier white wines, Fiano di Avellino. There are wonderful wines from Apulia made from the primary grapes of Negroamaro and Primitivo which is the grape believed to be the Genesis of Zinfandel.

You will find a nice array of wines coming from the island of Sardegna, from the white Vermentino's with their crisp clean make-up of fragrant floral aromas and ripe fruit in the palate, to the great reds made of Cannonau and Monica, the Big Bold wines made with the native Carrignan to Cabernet Sauvignon which grows exceedingly well on the island and comprises 100% of the great wine, Sella and Mosca "Marchese", along with the Vernaccia that's made in a sherry-like style, as well as some extraordinary desert wine made with Malvasia and Moscato.

Then last, but certainly not least in the south we have the wines from Sicily where the wines have made great strides in quality and worldwide popularity in the past few years. "Duca Enrico" and "Rosso del Conte" both made from 100% Nero d'Avola where for a long time, two of Sicily's small roster of prestigious wines, with few others. In the past few years, Sicily has seen a great boom in terms of quality, notoriety, and sales.

The Planeta family of Sicily has been one of the major forces in the recent trend of popularity and prestige of Sicilian wines. Planeta has skyrocketed to a well deserved fame in a very short amount of time, first with their big bold Merlot and Cabernet. In the past ten years their luscious Chardonnay has been ranked among the Top 50 Wines in the World. The Planeta's also produce a great wine made from Nero d' Avola and one from Syrah as well as the nice inexpensive white and red table wines Segreta, and my favorite Planeta Wine of all, their marvelous Cerasuolo di Vittoria, a wine that recently received the highly exalted DOCG status. All I can say is, this wine is yummy and goes well with any and all great Italian dishes

Another family who are very instrumental in the recent surge of Sicilian wines, is the Rallo family who have done a amazing job with their winery of Donnafugata. Most famous of the Donnafugata wines, would be the 100% Nero d' Avola based Mille una Notte, along with their highly touted desert wine "Ben Rye" Passito d' Panteleria on the Sicilian Island of Pantelleria, also famous for its Artists' Colony and for producing the best Capers in the World.

If you ever want to give yourself and your guests a "Special Treat" after dinner, pick up a bottle of Ben Rye and serve it after dinner. There is not a better way to "Guild the Lilly" of a fabulous meal than to finish it with a glass of Ben Rye which is literally like a Nectar of the Gods with wonderful taste of Honey Coated Peach and Apricots, it's sublime.

So, there you have it. If you want to go on the most incredibly diverse wine journey on Earth, dig into the wines of Italy.

WINES I'VE TASTED

My first forays into the world of wine were back in 1983. My cousin Tony and I would get together and drink a bottle or two of Gattinara and or Barolo, our favorite wines of the time. I was attending New York Technical College at the time for a degree in Hotel & Restaurant Management, but I was really there for the Culinary Arts program which was extensive and highly rated. The school had an incredible wine cellar and we often drank extraordinary old 1st Growth Bordeaux's and trophy Burgundy's. The most incredible tasting I've ever had in my life, and I've had many, was at New York Tech.

One night we had a 1947 Chateau Latour, a 1956 Cheval Blanc, a 1947 Petrus, and a 1959 Haute Brion, all of which were lovingly stored and in excellent condition. The wines were absolutely phenomenal.

I was hooked forever on the wonderful, magical, mystical World of Wine. I have been to many outstanding tastings and wine dinners over the years. I have to say, that great Bordeaux tasting is still unsurpassed. It is quite hard to top those vintages of the World's most prestigious wines, although my cousin Joe, with his fine collection has come close, as have some of the many fine Barolos, Barbarescos, Brunellos, Super Tuscans, and others I've tasted as the former Wine Director of Barbetta Restaurant on West 46th Street.

I have been a lucky benefactor of Joe's Macari's impressive collection and his great generosity of sharing them with myself, his wife Alexandra, wine-makers who have worked for him, visiting dignitaries of the Wine World, and a slew of others. Joe has a nice collection of Champagnes, Bordeaux's, Burgundy's both red and white, Barolo's, Amarone's, all the great Super Tuscan's, old vintage Porto, a few bottles of Vega Sicilia the greatest wine of Spain as well as being one of the World's greatest, along with the best wines from the Rhone and many trophy wines from California. As I've said Joe is very generous and often opens an amazing selection of wines when I cook dinner over his house or at Macari Vineyards. I have been fortunate to drink Chateau Lafite Rothchild 1961, 1963 Chateau d' Yquem, the great 1963 Crofts Vintage 1990, Chapoutier "La Turk" 1990, 1997 Saasicaia, Tignanello 1997, a marvelous 1990 Richbourg, a Bertani Amarone 1988, and Vega Sicilia "Unico" 1990, just to name a few of many incomparable wines.

I have had the Good Fortune to be invited to some Exclusive Lunches and Wine-Maker Dinners with the proprietors of a number of renowned wine estates.

In 1997 I was invited to one of my first Great Wine Luncheon. The Luncheon was held at Barolo Restaurant and was hosted by Antonella Bochino, the owner of the Contratto Wine Estate of Piemonte. We had a fantastic four course lunch in which we drank all the terrific Contratto wines. Antonella brought her excellent Gavi "Arnell", Barbera "Panta Rei," the famous "Solus Ad" one of the world's best. We had the extraordinary 1990 Barolo Cerecquio, and one of the finest sparkling wines I have ever tasted, which includes bottles of Crystal, Dom Perignon, Krug, Salon, Laurent Perrier, and Bilecart Salmon, some of the World's Great Champagne's, and the Conratto Brut 1990 could match and top most. This day we had the Contratto Brut 1990 which I will never forget. It was phenomenal, and easily ranked with Champagne's finest. The day was absolutely incredible, Phenomenal Wines that you just don't' get to drink every day, along with the owner of the Property, fine food and company.

Another special dinner in which I was one of only "Twelve Lucky Few" to receive an invitation to in October of 2002. This unforgettable wine dinner at Spark's Steakhouse (New York's Coolest), was hosted by Jacopo Biondi Santi, the great winemaker and co-proprietor of Biondi Santi. It was Jacopo's great grandfather who was the creator of the famed wine Brunello, almost 140 years previous in the Tuscan wine town of Montalcino.

Jacopo brought with him some of his best wines of the past ten vintages, and believe me, they were showing perfectly.

We started with a bottle of Sauvignon, followed by a Sassoloro 1998, Poggio Salvi Brunello 1995, the incredible Biondi Santi Brunello Greppone 1990, and a extraordinary Magnum of Schiodone 1995 it was a magical experience. The combination of drinking these great wines as Jacopo talked about each one, in the great steakhouse "Spark's," eating those mouth-watering Steaks and nice array of appetizers beforehand made for a combination of elements that could not be topped or duplicated anywhere. Imagine it, some of Italy's "Finest Wines," presented by the great Jacapo Biondi Sante at Sparks Steak House in New York City, "Wow, Wow, Wow," is all anyone can say. It was an outstanding evening that was completed with tasty deserts accompanied by the celebrated desert wine of Montalcino, Jacapo's example of Moscadello di Montalcino. The wine was lush and elegant.

The combination of all these great wines, eating some of the World's tastiest Steaks in Spark's, one of the World's best steakhouse's, while being hosted by a man who is the Great-Great-Grandson of the creator of Brunello, and who happens to be both a great winemaker and charming host. This was an unbeatable combination, a night I'll never forget.

I was proud and privileged to be invited to such a special occasion. Another memorable wine event I was fortunate to be invited to, was the press luncheon at Charlie Palmer's private dining room at the Design Center of New York when the Mondavi Family of California and the noble Florentine Family, The Frescobaldi's were introducing their collaboration of a wine they made in Montalcino called Lucente.

I was blessed to be among the fortunate few restaurant people as it was a "Press Luncheon" and there was only one table of restaurateurs that were invited.

The luncheon was hosted by Michael Mondavi and The Marchese Lamberto Frescobaldi who were both magnificent hosts. Charlie Palmers food was outstanding as were the wines we drank; Lucente, Mondavi Reserve Cabernet Sauvignon, and Castelllo Nipozzano Chianti Rufina Reserva 1993.

The Marchese Lamberto Frescobaldi and Michael Mondavi were impeccable host who gave eloquent speeches about their Wines, Vineyards and partnership and collaboration in making Luce and Lucente. We were given nice goody bags from the Marchese that contained a corkscrew, a beautiful book on Italian food and wine, and a bottle of their lush estate bottled olive oil. Could one possibly ask for more than a day like that, rubbing elbows with both American and Italian Wine Royalty? I think not!

The month of October, 2005 saw me sharing great food and wine with another famous Marchesi of wine, in none other than Marchesi Piero Antinori whose family has, like the Frescobaldi's been making Tuscan wine for more than 600 years. These two families are in fact the two most famous aristocratic families of wine in all of Italy, and to be one of the very few to be invited to such a small and prominent event, was again, quite an honor. The event was an incredible vertical tasting of Antinori's famed Tignanello, a Super Tuscan wine of great World renown. The tasting was held at the New York branch of the celebrated Italian wine bar restaurant, the Bottega del Vino of Verona, owned by Sevarino Barzan, who was in attendance along with some of the top people working for Antinori, some of New York's top Sommeliers and restaurateurs, and of course the esteemed Marchesi Piero Antinori himself.

The tasting was held in the impressive wine cellar of the Bottega del Vino on East 59th Street. I can't say that it was a once in a lifetime tasting, replace the word once with rare.Well, shall we say that it's not a tasting you'd see every day.

The tasting, was an impressive vertical array of 5 different vintages of Tignanello, consisting of the years 2001, 1999, 1997, 1995, and 1993. We also drank Solaia 2001, and Guado al Tasso 2001. "Quite a lineup."

The Marchesi gave a little synopsis on each vintage as we tasted from oldest to youngest. Needless to say, all the wines were wonderful. My favorite was no surprise, as I've always said that I thought the 1995 Tignanello was the best I have ever tasted. I have had, in fact every vintage of Tignanello from 1990-2001, excluding 1992 (Tignanello was not made in 1992), and including the 1988 which is was quite extraordinary. I hope I will get a chance to taste the 85, soon I hope as it is now around its peak.

Back to the 1995, like all of the wines we tasted that day, the color was deep and dark as though it were very young (a great sign). The nose was wonderful, consisting of casis and a beautiful aroma of dried figs and cherries which continued on the palate. The wine had great structure and a lengthy finish and was most enjoyable to drink. The Solaia and the Guado al Tasso, two of my favorites were also drinking quite well, though they are really made to drink with some age on them, as they pick up complexity and lovely exotic nuances. What can I say but that the tasting was outstanding. Another Memorable Day in my World of Wine.

In the year 2005, I found myself in another timely situation to taste 3 bottles of one of the most memorable wines I've ever had. What Wine? The 1973 vintage of Mastroberadino Taurasi Riserva, a most incredible wine. As the Wine Director at Barbetta Restaurant on West 46th Street in New York City from 2001 to 2005 I was the caretaker of one of the World's Greatest Italian Wine Cellars. Barbetta, in the year 2006 Celebrated its 100 Year Anniversary. The restaurant was founded at the turn of the century in 1906 by Sebastiano Maigolio. Sebastiano passed away in 1962 and his daughter Laura took over and transformed the restaurant from a very handsome establishment to New York's most lavish and elegant Italian Restaurant of its time. Laura was a trendsetter in many aspects of Italian Restaurants and Italian Wine in America. Among many of her first, she was one of the first to buy and sell wines by Angelo Gaja in the United States.

Laura is dedicated to making one of the greatest and most wonderful Italian Wine lists in the country. What she ended up creating was one of the "Top 5" Greatest Italian Wine Lists and Cellars in the entire World, and without a doubt the most extensive list of Vertical Flights of Single Vineyard Barolo and Barbaresco Crus in the entire World. Not even in

Piemonte where Barolo and Barbaresco come from, does there exist a Cellar that could match that of Barbetta's. "Quite a feat."

Anyway, trying to make a long story short, as the Wine Director/Sommelier at Barbetta for three years, I had the great fortune to touch, see, and taste some of the World's finest examples of Italian Wines. Great Barolos by the renowned Giacomo Conterno, Bruno Giacosa, Bartolo Mascarello, Bruno Cerretto, the House of Vietti, Angelo Gaja, and Aldo Conterno to name just a few. Also, I've tasted many of the famed Brunello Vintages of 1985, 88, 1990, 1997, and 1999 as well as all the renowned Super Tuscans of these years and other vintages as well.

Back to the 1973 Mastroberadino Taurasi Riserva. One night at Barbetta, a man was dining alone. We gave him the massive Barbetta Wine List. He studied it meticulously for about 15 minutes. He signaled to me that he was ready to order. His selection. "You guessed it, Mastroberadino Taurasi Riserva 1973. I went down to the cellar, picked the bottle and brought it upstairs. I presented it to the customer. At the ready, I had a large Bordeaux Glass, a Crystal Decanter, tasting glass, and my Corkscrew laid out on my serving cart. I screwed the screw into the cork and slowly and carefully pulled it up, being careful and hoping not to break the cork. Old corks can be very delicate. I slowly pulled up. The cork did not break. I brought the cork to my nose. It was fine. The wine had not gone bad (32 Years Old at the time of opening). It was more than fine. It smelled fabulous, and as I poured the wine from bottle to decanter, I couldn't believe my eyes. The color? It was amazing. Deep and dark, with hardly any loss of color tone. Barely any bricking or browning. For those of you who may not know, white wine darkens with age, while red wines do just the opposite, they lose color. This 1973 Mastroberadino Taurasi Reserva had almost no loss of color what-so-ever. This wine was a beautiful "Deep Dark Red Garnet."I couldn't believe my eyes. It was Phenomenal. I poured some in my tasting glass, looked at it in disbelief. Smelt it again, and then tasted.

"Wow!" It was beyond belief, full and delicious, packed with wonderful black fruit flavors of Currant and ripe Black Cherries with a bit of Exotic Spices and Far East Tea features. This may all sound a bit much for some, so all I can say is that 1973 Taurasi was just one of the tastiest most wonderful wines I have ever and probably "will ever" drink in my life. And I have had some great ones, but it just couldn't get any better. I primed the customer's glass and gave him a taste. He was flabbergasted to say the least. He Loved it. He told me he was born in 1973, it was his Birthday and he was treating himself. "Nice."

A few nights later, Adam Strum, the publisher of Wine Enthusiast Magazine was coming to dine at the restaurant. Wine Enthusiast had awarded us with its highest honor. We had been only one of two restaurants in New York, and just one of 16 in all of North America to win the prestigious Wine Enthusiast

Award of Ultimate Distinction and Mr. Strum, his wife and another couple were dining together at Barbetta. They were looking forward to a fine dinner of tasty food paired with Extraordinary Wines, so with Miss Laura's permission and insistence I selected some incredible wines for Mr. Strum and his party.

To start him off, I pulled a bottle of 1990 Bruno Giacosa Brut, a sparkling wine on par with any great French Champagne I've ever tasted, and I've tasted the Best. I followed the Giacosa Brut with a 1989 Giacomo Conterno Barolo Reserva Monfortino. If you had to pick just one out of all the great Single Vineyard Barolo Crus, many would put Giacomo Conterno Monfortino at the Top of The List, with the 1989 Vintage being one of the all-time-greatest. After the Monfortino, I served Mr. Strum's party the 1973 Mastroberadino Taurasi Riserva. Needless to say, "I blew his mind." It's rare to drink just one of these remarkable wines, let alone these three, even for a man like Mr. Adam Strum.

This is a small sample of what it was like to be the caretaker of one of the World's Great Italian Wine Lists, that of Barbetta Restaurant in New York. And let me tell you this, very few people know of it, and Miss Maigolio does not get anywhere near the credit she is due for creating and investing in such an incredible Cellar, it's remarkable.

NO TROTA in BARDOLINO

In the Spring of 2001 I took a most wonderful Wine trip. An Italian Wine Trip. I had been on a couple of these trips before, but this was one turned out to be extra special.

My cousin Joe Macari and I had planned it for several months. We would go to VinItaly, the World's largest wine exposition. Vinitaly is thee Italian Wine exposition that takes place every April in the Italian fair city of Verona. It's a five day affair of Italian Wine, Italian Food, Italian Wine, and more Italian Wine. It was going to be a blast, but things came up and Joe was not able to make it. So my good friend Jimmy Starace took Joe's place.

We were unable to fly over together as I was flying on Tuesday and Jimmy had to shoot a Scotch Commercial that very day. I flew Swiss Air to Venice with a stop at Zurich in-between where I picked up a box of nice Cuban Cigars and some Chocolates in the airport.

I arrived at Marco Polo International Aero Porto after a 50 minute flght from Zurich, took the water-taxi to Piazza San Marco, hopped a Vaporetto to the Rialto from which point I walked a couple blocks to one of my favorite hotels in Venice, The Albergo Guerrato. Guerrato is a charming little place I discovered on an exploratory trip to Venice in April of 1995. The location of this hotel is incredible. It is literally in the heart of the famous Rialto Market, which has been in continuous operation for over Six Hundred Years. The market purveys the freshest fish, fruits, vegetables, meat, and poultry to the citizens and Restaurateurs of Venice. If you walk out the door of Guerratto and take a right-hand-turn, walk a mere 10 feet, you will be Smack Dab in the Middle of the World's greatest, most interesting food market of all, the "Rialto of Venice."

In the Rialto, you will find thee most fantastic assortment of Sea Creatures of every size, shape, and color imaginable, and ones you've never even dreamed of. They are there. "It's amazing!" One of the most wonderful of sights in La Serenisima, and just like walking into St. Marks Square, it is absolutely free.

It is quite an adventure just walking around the market, seeing all the vibrant colors of the fruits and vegetables, scoping the various types of fish, Shrimp, Crabs, Mussels, Clams (Vongole), and all other Sea Creatures. You walk, watch, and listen to the sounds of the Rialto, the Merchants of Venice yelling and singing as they hawk their many wares. "Carciofi,

Carciofi, Scampi, Tutti Pesci, Polpo, Polpetti Fresca!"
It is quite the spectacle.

So I arrived at Guerrato, checked in and took a quick shower to refresh and revive. I had to get out, take a nice little walk around the "Magical City." Along the way I'd have some Cichetti and a glass of local wine, maybe a nice Cabernet Franc. Speaking of Cabernet Franc, quite a lot of it is grown in North-Eastern Italy, especially in the Veneto and Friulli as well. So much is grown that many wine bars and restaurants in and around Venice serve Cab Franc as the house red. Imagine that. Yes it's a big local variety. I might have a glass of Cab Franc or maybe I'd drink the Valpolicella from one of my friends, either, the Valpolicello Classico from Allegrini, Zenato's Ripassa, or "Brolo" from the esteemed House of Masi.

I stop at the first nice Bacaro I come across and order a some Cichetti of little fried Meatballs, Melanzane al Forno, some grilled Calamaris, and little Gamberetti dressed in lemon and olive oil. I followed this nice little plate of Cichetti with a tasty Spaghetti Vongole and yes I did drink some of the fine Cab Franc of the Veneto. By the way, Bacarois the Venetian dialect for wine bar, which translates to House of Bacchus, the Roman God of Wine.

I had the most amazing time as always, walking through the labyrinth that is Venice, through this calle (sidewalks) and that, along the fondamentas (walkways next to canals), and up and over one beautiful little bridge after the other. Venice has some 450 of "them," bridges that is. Checking out all the whimsical Mask Shops (Mascara), art galleries, fantastic print shops, and shops that make exquisite hand-made writing paper. You'll find fine clothing stores, pastry shops, trattorias, ristorante, Wine Bars (Bacari), and all manner of shops selling antiques, Murano Glass, Lace from Burano, Italian ceramics, and all sorts of astonishing little trinkets and things. It's a shoppers Paradise, Venice.

After making that long journey from the great city of New York, having lunch and taking a long walk, exploring Venice once again, I was a bit tired so I made my way back through the maze of Venezia to The Albergo Guerrato. I needed a little nap.

I awoke after a hour and a half, took another shower, then made my way over the Rialto Bridge to San Polo and had dinner at a nice little Trattoria. My dinner started with an Antipasto Misto de Mare that consisted of tiny little Adriatic Shrimp, Crab Salad, and Sarde en Soar. I followed the antipasto with a perfect bowl of Spaghetti Nero (Spaghetti with Squid Ink and Squid) while drinking some tasty Venica Tocai.

The dinner was excellent. I didn't have any dessert. I strolled back to Guerrato to sleep the night away and Dreaming of the Mystical Magical City.

The next day I arose early as I always do when I'm in Europe. Do not want to waste any precious time. I had a my nice little Guerratto Breakfast in the charming dining room that looks like it has been stuck in a Venetian time warp from the 1920's. Very young considering that the whole of Venice is a "800 year old time warp." This dining room is really cool, with its terrazzo floor, old Paintings & Photographs, and a beautiful ornate credenzas and mirrors from the 20's. Did you know, "Mirrors" were invented in Venice and that the process of making them was "Top Secret?"

The Guerrato Breakfast consist of a perfect Cappuccino ("you've never tasted one so good"), apricot yogurt, a Cornetto (a Italian Croissant), a banana, and some delicious fresh squeezed Blood Orange juice from Sicily. "Yum!"

After breakfast I went wandering around Venice, shopping, taking lots of pictures, and making wonderful new discoveries every couple of minutes or so.

I had a marvelous lunch at Harry's Bar, of Beef Carpaccio and Tagiolini, washed down with a couple of Harry's famed Bellinis, then I wandered over to one of the World's great caffe's to rendezvous with my bud Jimmy. Our designated meeting time was

242

1:30 PM at Florian's Caffe, smack right dab in the middle of the Piazza San Marco, the World's most beautiful square. Florian's has served the likes of Antonio Vivaldi, Napoleon, Churchill, Hemingway, Katherine Hephurn, Verdi, and Wagner since Florian first opened the caffe doors way back in 1720, and the place has been going strong ever since. Just a few years until they celebrate their 300 Year Anniversary. That's Venice for you, they have a place where you can go for an Espresso, Cappuccino, Prosecco, or Campari, and this place (Florian's) has been operating for close to 300 years. Besides serving you, over the years they have served Kings, Queens, Presidents, Prime Minesters, Princes, Princesses, Rock-Stars, Movie Stars, you and me, everybody and anybody. That's Florian's.

I sat at a table outside under the portico at Florian. Jimmy arrived on time, and we relaxed with a couple Negronis before lugging his bags over to the hotel.

That night we had a nice dinner of antipasto of shrimp, mussels, and razor clams, followed by some Gnocchi Pomodoro. We drank a bottle of local Refosco at a cool little trattoria near in the Rialto.
The next day we arose early to have our Guerrrato breakfast before heading to the Santa Lucia Stazzione to catch the train to Verona and Vinitaly.
It's a quick hour and fifteen minutes by train

from Venice to Verona, home of Romeo and Julietta, Gnocchi, and Italy's Greatest and most famous Wine Bar, the Bottega del Vino. Verona is also home to one of the World's best preserved Roman Arenas, and Vinitaly, the World's largest wine exposition of all. From the train station we caught a local bus to the show.

Vinitaly was great. First, we walked about for a few minutes before we came across the booth of my friend Anna, whose family makes Prima Uva Brandy. Prima Uva is a Brandy that is served like Grappa, though technically it is Brandy. We sat down for a few minutes to chat and drink a bit of the Prima Uva.

I was trying to meet up with my friend Pietro Cavallo who's a representative for Donna Fugatta, Fatttoria Barbi, and Fontana Fredda. We kept missing him as we went to each booth.

We went over to the Fattoria Barbi exhibit looking for Pietro. He was not there so we visited with Serena Columbini whose husband's family owns Barbi, one of the oldest producers of Brunello in Montalcino. We drank a good bit of their fine Brunello while munching on their delicious Salami that they make on their estate. We had a great time hanging out with Serena, she has a marvelous personality as most people in the wine business do. In actuality, it seems as though the proprietors of most vineyards are exceptionally warm and friendly people, and Serena certainly fits the mold. We thoroughly enjoyed Serina's warm hospitality. It was a memorable visit munching on their tasty Home-Made Salami while sipping their renowned Brunello, coupled with the presence of the always bright and charming Serena.

We were quite happy with our good fortune to be being entertained so wonderfully by the owners of one of the oldest and most celebrated Houses of Brunello in the World, Fattoria Barbi. It may be a cliché, but it is oh-so-true, "It just doesn't get any Better than That!"

Speaking of warm wonderful people who own vineyards, we went over to the Terrabianca booth to visit with good friend Roberto Gundelar. When I say booths, sometimes they are booths, while others like Terrabianca's are almost like you're in the home of the producer (producers being the Proprietors of a wine estate). We sat with Roberto and his daughter Maya for a nice half hour visit. We chatted as Roberto took us through the Terrabianca line-up of Chardonnay, Croce (Chianti), Fonte, and one of my favorites "Cipresso" made with 100% Sangiovese.

Of course we had the famous Super Tuscan "Campaccio" made with 70% Sangiovese and 30% Cabernet Sauvignon, a great bottle of wine. As

Roberto poured each wine for us, telling us about each one, the time came for a new Super Tuscan they had just come out with, "Cepate" made with Merlot and Cabernet Sauvignon, it is a qualified knockout, blockbuster wine that can compete with the World's best. The wine is packed with incredible lush fruit from vines that have very low concentrated yields. It's a powerhouse to say the least.

As I must often say, simply because I'm put into so many memorable occasions, "It doesn't get much better than this." Drinking some of the World's great wines, which are being poured by the man that produces them as he explains each one to you, personally entertaining you. Can you beat that? Again, my pal Jimmy was astonished at the graciousness of such a renowned host and my good fortune to have such special relationships with so many prominent people of Italian Wine World.

We finished the tasting with Roberto's fine Vin Santo before going on our merry way. Over to the Zenato booth to see Nadia Zenato who as many girls of family's who own wine estates in Italy, she handles promotions and marketing for the winery. Her father Sergio makes their famed Amarone along with a truly fine Ripasso.

We visited a number of friend's booths in the two days we were at Vinitaly, including Alesandro Landini of Fattoria Vitticio, Antonio Rallo of

Donnafugata, and Giannpaulo Venica, whose family makes some of Italy's very best white wines, including their prodigious Tocai and famed Sauvignon Blanc, Ronco d' Mele, "The Hill of Apples."

The best things about being at Vinitaly are not being at the show itself, which to sum up in a nutshell is to be up on the latest happenings in the Italian Wine World, to smooze with the Italians as well as your peers from New York or wherever you may be from. Speaking of New York, by far the largest foreign contingent of people from anywhere around the globe at Vinitaly, is the contingent from New York. This is one aspect that appeals to a New York Italian Wine Guy, such as myself. Hanging out in Verona, in Italy, at Vinitaly; conducting business, tasting wine (of Course), eating wonderful Italian food, and having a good time. Well it's not all fun and games. It's actually quite grueling. You get up early in the morning, have breakfast, then make your way to the exposition, Vinitaly. Most will get there sometime between 10:30 and 11:30 AM. You go from booth to booth. You taste wine, an average of about 70 in a day. At some booths you may not know anyone there, this can be good. You will know people at some of the other booths and at these ones you might spend fifteen, twenty, maybe even thirty minutes with your friends, chatting, tasting, socializing. Having friends and hanging out with them has its good points and bad ones. The bad point is that you spend a lot of time with them and less time seeing other things, especially when you visit with numerous friends all in one day. The good points are obvious. Number one, you are not treated like just another "Joe Smoe." Actually, you're usually treated like a King. You don't stand in front of the counter tasting with the masses. You sit with the owner at a table. You relax and are given a great deal of attention, tasting their fine wine, getting little snacks, maybe some homemade Salami and Cheese from the estate's private stock. It's quite a lot of fun, being treated so royally. Who doesn't like that? So I may be I'm a little vain? Isn't everyone? "Sue me!"

So you socialize with the "Big Shots," and you make plans to go visit vineyards after the exposition is over. Here, again, the "Red Carpet" will be rolled out, and you will be treated Royally touring their Estate. These are some of the best aspects for going to Vinitaly. Also, just the fact of being there, it gives you more cachet amongst your peers as well as the producers (Vineyard owners) that you buy wine from. Each trip also adds to your personal bonds with others and increases your life's experiences with memories of grand times. Not so bad?

After being in Verona a couple of days, doing Vinitaly, going to the famous wine bar Bottega del Vino where the Italian Wine World meets. You have a few nice meals in varios trattorias, as well as eating tasty Porchetta Sandwiches outside the fair grounds, it was time to leave.

It wasn't easy, but we left the fair city of Verona, the Roman Arena, Bottega del Vino, Romeo and Julietta. We made our way to Lago di Garda for a day of checking out the Valpolicella Classico region, the place that makes the renowned wines of Amarone, Bardolino, Valpolicella, and Recioto de Valpolicella. We were in for another treat. Amarone, one of Italy's most prestigious wines is made in a very special and unique manner were by the best grapes in the vineyard (Corvina, Rondinella, and Molinara) are picked and then dried on racks for two to three months before being vinified into wine. This process reduces the water content of the grapes and intensifies the flavors of which you get figs, raisons, and prunes, over ripe fruit of bitter cherries and perhaps a touch of dark chocolate. Amarone is one of the World's premier wines and here we were in its domain, ready to explore and drink of this fine nectar with some of the top producers of this one of the World's most celebrated wines, Amarone and it's most renowned porducers of the wine; Masi,

Dal Forno, Qunitarelli, Allegrini, Zenato, Bertani, and others. This people, is pure bliss.

We had breakfast in a grand caffe at the water's edge, in the town of Garda on the picturesque shores of Lake Garda. The Alps shooting up majestically in the background was quite a sight, beautiful.

After breakfast, we stopped in at a local butcher shop and bought Speck and some of the famous local olive oil, which is one of the World's most northerly produced olive oils in the world. We then hopped back into the Scotto Fabio and drove all around the zone of Valpollicella. We drove high up into the mountains and stopped in at a wine bar that was on top of some mountain that had a beautiful view of Lake Garda and the valley below. We drank Tocai, and I'm certain in this remote location that we were probably the only Americans to have ever stepped foot inside this rural little bar. We were looking for the legendary Giuseppe Quintarelli whose vineyard is in the small town of Negar, high up into the mountains. His wines are at the pinnacle of the great Amarone Sphere, and Giuseppe is the God of Amarone and the region (Kingdom) of Valpolicella Classico.

Quintarelli's legendary wines are produced in small quantities and are very hard to come by, either in Italy or in the States, and if you do find them and would like to possess them, you must pay dearly, not with your life, but with some cold hard cash. Giuseppe and his vineyard are mysterious and mystical, and I guess it should not have been a surprise to us that although we were in the town of Negar and asking the locals how to get there, nobody knew who he was or where the vineyard was located. I found out a year later that the locals are tired of people asking them how to get to the Quintarelli estate. They don't even want to help a poor stranger out, so they lie and say "No," they don't know where he is or how to get to the vineyard. "Ce la Vei." Not long after this, there was a picture in the Wine Spectator or some other magazine that was of a house in Negar with a sign that the owners put up that read "Quintarelli is Not Here." You see?

Although we drove all around Negar, and tried our best to find Giuseppe, we couldn't.It just wasn't in the cards.

So we made our way over to the beautiful estate of Serego Alighieri which is owned and operated by descendants of the famed Florentine Poet, author of The Devine Comedy, Dante Alighieri. The property is gorgeous and in no way second-fiddle to Quintarelli, and as the years pass, and I get a little wiser, I have come to know and love the Amarone of Serego Aligieri even more. Along with the Amarone made by Sergio Zenato, they are my own two personal favorites.

We toured the vineyards and cellars filled with rare Cherry Wood Cask. We savored the excellent Valpolicella and Amarone in the tasting-room, and before we left, we picked up a few bottles of their fine wine to bring back to New York to drink at one of our celebrated dinner parties.

The Amarone's of Serego Aliigheri are some of the finest, most wonderful Amarone's in the whole zone of Valpolicella Classico (the only area in the World where Amarone is made). They are aged in large the rare Cherry-Wood Cask, which give these wonderful wines unique aging characteristic, as the pores of

The thing that makes barrels and cask made Cherry Wood different than those of oak is that the pores of Cherry Wood are a bit larger than those of oak, which helps the wine mature a bit faster than oak does, thus making a 6 year old wine taste more like a mature 7 years of age.

Something I'd like to say about the wines of Valpolicella. Because of the fact that Valpolicella, along with Bardolino, and Soave became so comercial and popular (too popular) in the United States back in the 1970's because the firm of Bolla and a few other producer were making it in mass quantities, marketing, and selling millions of bottles every year, and selling it through massive TV Ad campaigns, these wines lost all respect from wine drinkers and the Wine World. They were looked down upon in disdain for over twenty years. It is true that for a time there were very few producers of good quality Valpolicella, Bardolino, and Soave. This region on a whole has made a tremendous turn around in terms of making really excellent quality wines of Valpolicella and Soave, while the Amarone's have always maintained their great eminence. If you are someone who is 50 years old or older and haven't had any Soave or Valpolicello of late, please do give them a try. They are quite good.

There are now excellent examples of Soave (Pieropan and Anselmi), Valpolicella (Allegrini and Quinterelli), and Valpolicella Ripasso (Bertani, Zenato, Masi) being produced in this zone, but it has been difficult for this area to overcome the stigma it gained from the mediocrity of the seventies and into the eighties. I myself, did champion these wines along with Morrelino d'Scansano and Tocai of which I was one of the first big sellers in America at my former Wine Bar in New York City, Bar Cichetti.

We drove back to Lake Garda to the town of Bardolino. I had told Jimmyboy earlier in the day that fresh local Lake Trout was the dish to eat in this area, as no matter where you are traveling in the world; you should always eat the most famous local dishes. We arrived at Bardolino around Three o'clock

253

in the afternoon and were salivating for some of that famous Lake Trout, sautéed in butter with lemon and parsley. That would really hit the spot, along with a nice bottle of local Soave. Our desire for the tasty Trota was not to be fulfilled. Not that day. By the time we got into town, every restaurant in Bardolino was closed. Not one was open for business. Most restaurants in Italy close for two to three hours between lunch and dinner but you can usually find a couple that stay open continuously, but no, not in this town. Jimmy was fuming. He wanted his Trota! He was really peeved, almost throwing a minor fit.

The only thing we could find open was a caffe. I settled for a pannino and Jimmy got some gelato, but he was not a happy camper, he wanted his lake trout. We had to make our way south towards Tuscany, so we hopped in the car and as we were driving out of the lakeside town of Bardolino we were shouting out the window at the people on the street, "No Trota! No Trota!!" I know, it sounds kind of silly and sophomoric, but it was actually very funny as we yelled, "No Trota, No Trota!!!" and watched all the funny stunned expressions on people's faces as they were yelled at by two "Crazy Americans" driving in a Scotto Fabia yelling, "No Trota, No Trota!!!" As they say, "You had to be there."

Driving down south we decided to stay overnight in Bologna. We got two huge rooms in the hotel that I stayed in the other time I was in Bologna in 1995, "The Palace Hotel." I would end up staying in this hotel for a third time, when a few years later I went to Vinitaly with cousins Tony nad Joe.

That night we finally got one good meal for the day. We found a nice restaurant a few blocks from the hotel. We had mixed Salumi and roast peppers for the Antipasto. For the secondo (main course), Jimmy had a Veal Milanese while I opted for the Bolito Misto, the famous Northern Italian dish of mixed boiled meats. Bolito Misto taste infinitely better than it sounds. The meats vary according to each individual who prepares the dish. The one I had this time in Bologna contained in it; Cotechino the famed Sausage of Emilia Romagna, Beef Tongue, and Beef Short Ribs. Jimmy looked at it and thought I was out-of-my-mind for eating it. We drank some local Sangiovese with the meal. Everything was quite nice and it took some of the sting out of the fact that we had, "No Trota," in Bardolino.

The next day we got up early, had breakfast, and headed towards The Chianti Classico Region, driving along the Autostrada, paying numerous costly road tolls as we went along.

We decided to stop in Florence for lunch. We parked the car at the train station near Santa Maria

Novella and scouted the area for a good place to eat. We found a great little trattoria where we ate the quintessential Tuscan Antipasto of Crostini Toscano (Chicken Liver Pate on toasted Tuscan Bread). We both followed the Crostini with Paparadelle with Rabbit Sauce, another Tuscan specialty. And we drank a couple of glasses of nice local Chianti Fiorentino, "Tasty." We finished the meal with biscotti and some excellent Vin Santo. It was a nice little meal in a charming Old Trattoria. The Lunch we thoroughly enjoyed.

After lunch Jimmy and I hopped back in the little rented car and to make the last leg of the journey to Chianti Classico. The region of Chianti starts at its northern end just a few miles south of Florence, while the southern most part ends at Castelnuovo Barendenga, a few miles north of Siena.

We drove south out of Firenze to catch the Ancient Roman Road known as the Chiantiagana. Imagine that, the Romans built this road some 2000 years ago, and here we are, more than 2000 years later driving our rented Scotto Fabia on it into the Heart of the Chiant Classico Zone. We drove down through Prunetto, Greve, and into the lovely town of Panzano, of some storied Chianti and Italy's Rock-Star Butcher, "Dario Cecchini. We stayed at The Albergo Valle which is situated in one thee most beautiful spots in all of Chianti Classico on one of the highest points in Panzano overlooking several other vineyards with thousands of rows of the wonderful Sangiovese vines. There is also a wonderful vantage point of seeing the center of the village of Panzano right out the back window of my hotel room. This incredible view looked over the estates vineyards of Fattoria Valle with Panzano not too far in the background. It was some site to wake up to in the morning. I arose early in the morning, and would go and sit on the terrazzo in back of the hotel, relaxing and taking in the gorgeous site before my blessed eyes.

I gazed these splendid estates with their rows and rows of Vines of Sangiovese, Olive Tree groves, with cypress trees that seemed as though they were plucked down strategically by "God" himself on the crest of almost every other hill in the region. There are castles, beautiful villas, rugged old stone farm houses, picturesque gardens and all the happenings of an early morning day in the Chianti Classico. It is a site to behold, and just to impossible for mere words to ever dream of explaining. You just have to see it for yourself.

How wonderful it was to be in that land with its incomparable scenery, among the wine, the vines, the rolling hills, winding country roads that lead from one stunning wine estate to another, that contain thousands of small oak barrels filled with incredible Super Tuscan wines, while the larger, more majestic Slovenian Oak Barrels are filled to the brim with the famed, "Chianti!" It is truly a magical place to be. Dare I say, "Heaven on Earth."

The Fattoria Valle is a fantastic little winery that makes Chianti Classico in the classic way, made up of 95% Sangiovese with 5% Cannaiolo and not a trace of any dreaded Merlot or Cabernet Sauvignon, has its place, but not in Chianti. This Chianti is rustic and tasty with lovely bitter cherry and a touch of spice on the palate. The wine is of medium body, not too concentrated, which is the way true classic old-style Chianti should be, and there is nothing like drinking such a wine right on the property it is produced on, "The ultimate of the wine drinking experience."

The Albergo Valle is an incredibly beautiful old stone building in which the walls are sixteen inches thick. The guest rooms are all impeccably decorated, with antique furniture and beautiful paintings.

You enter the building into a stunning foyer with a Carrera Marble floor, crystal chandelier, and lovely antique furniture, and paintings of great taste.

There are four common rooms on the first floor off the foyer. There are two sitting rooms filled with wonderful chairs, sofas, and love seats, along with fine prints and paintings. There is a billiard room as well as a charming bar room where you can purchase some of the great wines of the region. It was wonderful to sit and chat with the proprietors and other guest while drinking much tasty Valle Chianti.

There is also a fine little restaurant at Valle that serves superb local dishes. We had a delicious meal there one night, consisting of; Crostini Toscana, Salumi, Raviolis, and Bistecca. Everything was perfectly prepared and the bottle of Valle Chianti was the perfect pairing of wine.

If all this was not enough to ask for, and you certainly you think it would be, two of Italy's most renowned Salumeria's are in the area. One is, Dario Cecchini the "Crazy Singing Butcher" of Panzano and the other is Forloni in the center of Greve the town next to Panzano. Add to this estates like Castello Rampalo, Castello Querceto, Fontodi, Nozzole, and Verazzano to name but a very few of many outstanding wine properties. "If you're into great food and wine, this is your proverbial 7th Heaven."

I am quite lucky to have amazing wine connections in Italy. I have friends who own vineyards in every corner of the country; in Friuli, Sicily, The Veneto, Campania, and Tuscany, all over. These friendships give me special access to many vineyards, getting the Red Carpet Treatment as I visit all the various estates. I'm treated to private tours of the vineyards and cellars conducted by the winemakers and property owners. We taste wines that are still in the barrel, and to have lunches and dinners at these place with the owners of the estates is really something special. Each and every one.

The first friend that I went to visit on this particular trip to Chianti Classico was Alesandro Landini the proprietor of Fattoria Viticcio in Greve. Alesandro took us for a tour around his vineyard on which you can see the famed wine estates of Castello Verrazzano and Vichomaggio in the near distance. These two castles are each atop a hill with a valley in-between.

Alessandro took us through his cellars where we tasted his Chianti, and Super Tuscan wines Monile and Pruniao. Prunaio made 100% Sangiovese Grosso is one of my favorites. Pruniao has the perfect balance of power and finesse at a very fair price compared to many of the other famous Super Tuscan wines, and it is made with the help of   one of Italy's greatest winemakers, Vittorio Fiore.

Alessandro showed us some of the rooms he was restoring in one of the old stone buildings for guests to rent.

We finished up our visit with some of the lush Viticcio Vin Santo, took a few pictures with Alessandro, and said our goodbyes till next time as we left for our next stop.

From Viticcio it was a short ten minutes to visit Cavaliere Luigi Cappellini, the proprietor of Castello Verrazzano, the estate where the explorer Verrazzano the discoverer of New York harbor was born in the castle in 1485. Verrazzano in Greve is one of the most beautiful wine estates in the World whether you're in Piemonte, Bordeaux, Burgundy, Chile, Spain, Napa, or Sonoma you will not find a property more beautiful and enchanting as that of Castello Verrazzano. The castle itself was a Roman and Etruscan installation long before the Verrazzano family obtained the land. It was once of strategic military importance to Florence when that city was at war with the Sienese and others. Verrazzano dominated the Greve Valley which is about 18 miles south of Florence.

The castle is situated on the highest part of the property which is more than 600 acres in total area. The beautiful vineyards fall down from the heights There are also marvelous Olive Tree Groves as well as pear and apple orchards on the property. In addition to the fabulous wines, The Verrazzano Estate produces excellent olive oil, one of the finest Red Wine Vinegars you could ever imagine, Baslamic Style Vinegar Aceto), and lavender scented honey. There are also exquisite formal gardens on the grounds behind the castle itself. Looking at all the surrounding scenery from this vantage point, well, the setting is beyond compare.

The management has put together a wonderful tour of the castle and its cellars that are conducted by Gino Rossi and the rest of his staff of friendly informative guides who have numerous facts and antidotes about the history of the castle, the family, and the surrounding area as well as basic general information about Chianti, wine and how it's made.

There's also a big beautiful dining room in the castle where the general public can partake of the marvelous experience it is of eating a meal at magnificent wine estate. People enjoy a wonderful Tuscan meal of assorted Antipasti, Pasta, roasts meats, grilled fish, and desserts accompanied by Chianti, Super Tuscan's, and Vin Santo from the Verrazzano Estate.

Having lunch or dinner in this castle on this incomparable wine estate, eating on the terrace or in the main dining room with the spectacular view, it's an unbeatable combination, and one that not many ever have the pleasure to experience. If, you can, do not pass the chance to do it yourself.

One fine example of the connections that give me special inside entry to private tours, tastings, parties, lunches, and dinners with the winemakers or the proprietors of wine estates around the world would be a fabulously memorable lunch I had with Conti Sebastiani Capponi and his brother Conti Nicolo Capponi at their families estate in Greve, Italy, the Villa Calcinaia which was purchased by the noble Capponi family in 1524. Villa Calcinaia was once a Florentine outpost on the medieval road of Greve.

The Capponi's have been producing wonderful wine, olive oil, and vinegars since the Renaissance. I will always remember the lunch I shared with Conti Sebastiani and Nicolo Capponi one beautiful Spring day a few years back. Nicolo gave us a whimsical tour of the vineyards and its cellars. We first started in the beautiful old kitchen of the villa which apart from the gas stove looks almost exactly as it has for over 500 years, incredible. Before we started on our sojourn of the cellars of Villa Calcinaia, Niccolo treated us to some the extraordinary Salami and Prosciutto that they make on the estate solely for Capponi family consumption as well as any guest who are lucky enough to partake as well. It was quite an especially unique treat, eating the private artisanal Capponi family Salumi while sipping their superb Chianti in the medieval kitchen as the house cook was grilling veal in the ancient fireplace which would be part of our special lunch to come.

Niccolo then took us through the labyrinth of the the Calcinaia Cellars and into a room where the Capponi's have a 300 year old mother. Yes that's right, a "300 Year Old Mother!" A "Mother" is the starting process of making vinegar and it can be kept alive indefinitely, thus in this case for the past 300

263

years, so they say. The vinegar it produces is exceptional.

Niccolo then led us into the adjacent room and proclaimed, "These are from Ali Baba." They were large terra cotta vessels where the estate olive oil is stored, and they do look like they came from the caves of Ali Baba himself.

The Count (Conti) then led the way to the fermentation room where the pressed grapes are turned into the famed wine of Chianti and Vin Santo.

From the fermentation room we went into the cellars where Chianti was being aged in large Slovenian Oak Cask. We took a barrel samples out of the cask of 1994 Chianti Reserva and the 1995 Chianti Classico. Tasty!

After barrel-tasting the Chianti, Niccolo brought us into the room where thousands of bunches of Trebbiano grapes were hanging from nails on beams so they could dry out before being turned into the lush nectar of Tuscan Vin Santo which we would be drinking later on to finish off our unforgettable lunch.

Conti Niccolo then led us outside to the Capponi vineyards and to their herb and vegetable garden in back of the castle.

After seeing the garden and walking through the vines of Sangiovese we joined up with Niccolo's brother Conti Sebastiani Capponi in a beautiful little dining room for our incredible lunch to come.

The dining room was decorated in the perfect combination of country elegance of which was unchanged for some 500 years.

We started this wonderful meal with an antipasto misto of Crostini Toscano, Prosciutto, and roast peppers. The antipasto was followed by a simple but tasty Rigatoni Pomodoro. We were served the Veal that we had observed being roasted by the cook previously, along with some sautéed escarole from the garden.

We then followed the Veal with some Pecorino Toscano while enjoying the Capponi's great Chianti throughout the meal.

For desert we ate succulent Oranges while sipping on the extraordinary Calcinaia Vin Santo which to me is the best expression of this famous Tuscan dessert wine that I have ever tasted, ever better than the superb Avognesi Vin Santo 1990 which received the highest score possible for any wine, a 100 from the Wine Spectator. The Vin Santo from Villa Calcinaia is perfectly balanced with the sweetness of ripe Pears and Apricots, with hints of Wild Flowers and Walnuts and at the finish, utterly Perfecto!

This meal was one of the most memorable of my life, dining with the Capponi's in a lovely dining room in the Castel which dates back to the Renaissance, at the Villa Calcinaia in the heart of Chianti Classico, drinking their fabulous wine with our meal, it was an experience that not many people ever get the chance to do, simply extraordinary.

On the third day in Panzano we went to visit the stunning wine estate of Vignamaggio. This estate has quite a history behind it. La Gioconda (Mona Lisa) was born at this stately villa, and the painting is believed to been painted by DaVinci on the grounds of Vignamaggio.

The estate is absolutely beautiful. If you look at the background of the painting Mona Lisa you will get an idea of the beauty of the estate and the panoramas you see from its various vantage points, they are spectacular.

If you'd like to get a more indebt look at what the estate looks like and you can't make it to Greve, rent the movie "Much Ado About Nothing" by Kenneth Brannagh. The movie was shot on the estate. The winemaker Antonio gave us a nice tour of the grounds and cellars as we tasted the Chianti Classico, Vin Santo, their Super Tuscan Obsession, and the Chianti Classsico Reserva "Mona Lisa."

After our visit to Vignamaggio we had lunch in a nice little enotecca in the center of Greve. We had some excellent Salumi to start, followed by some tasty Lasagna al Forno, and treated ourselves to a bottle of Cenattoia Chianti Riserva 1997. This smart little wine bar had a warm ambiance with very good food and great wines which were available of course to drink on the premises as well as being available to buy on a retail level. I wish we could do that in New York. As we were enjoying our Lasagna I noticed a bottle of Il Carbonaione on one of the shelves. We had an extensive agenda of vineyards to visit and the Fiore's were not on my list. When I saw the bottle of this renowned Super Tuscan I figured since we were in Greve, why not visit the Fiore's at Podere Scalette, so I tried to call Roberto Fiore to see if we could stop by. One of the guys behind the bar of the enoteca was kind enough to help us with the call. He got the number and made the call. The phone rang and when someone picked up on the other end, it was "The Maestro" himself, Vittorio Fiore who happens to be along with Franco Barnabei and Giacomo Tachis, one of Italy's three most exalted and famous winemakers. Besides making his own wine Vittorio is the consulting winemaker for a number of other top wine estates in Tuscany. He is highly sought after.

We were given directions to Podere Scallette which is in the hamlet of Ruffoli within Greve. We were driving for a little while when Jimmy said, "Let's go back, I don't think we're going to find it."

I said, "Let me go another mile or two." No sooner were the words out of my mouth when I saw the sign for the winery and said, "there it is! Podere Scallette. This is it."

We parked the car and looked around to see who was there. At first we didn't see anyone. Suddenly a wonderful little old man appeared and started talking to us. Well, actually through sign-language and the limited amount of Italian that we knew, we managed to communicate a bit. The little old man's name was Dante. He was a beautiful 85 year old wonder who lived in Ruffoli his entire life. We were told by Yjuri that Dante had never traveled any further from Greve than to Florence (18 miles), and this he only did a handful of times in his life.

We told Dante that we were from New York and asked him if he had ever been there. He replied waving his hands across each other as if to say no, then he stomped his foot to the ground that he had never left while he grunted, "Ughh, Uggh, Ugh" and pointed his finger to the ground. We had a great time trying to converse with Dante for about twenty minutes while we waited for Yjuri and Mr. Fiore to arrive. They were doing a little work in the vineyard and would be coming soon. We were in no hurry, Dante was keeping us more than entertained. Maybe we should put him on film. The man is thoroughly charming, funny too.

Podere Scallette is located way up on the highest point in Greve and commands a fantastic on which you can see the whole zone of Chianti Classico inbetween the cities of Florence and Siena. Standing there on the Fiore wine estate you get what has to be one of the World's most spectacularly beautiful panoramic, views. The rolling Tuscan hills that are quilted with millions of rows of lush grapevines, fruit orchards, olive groves with thier silvery-greenish leaves of these trees, winding country roads, palatial estates, castles, farmhouses, woods, villages, and the many Cypress Trees.

The complex of small buildings that comprise the winery and the Fiore home are on either side of the road. From this point the vineyard sweeps down steep slopes with rows of some of the finest Sangiovese vines in the on Earth. The vines are over 40 years old. The Fiore's also have a bit of Merlot planted on their vineyard. With the Merlot they make a small production of a wine exclusively for the Enotecca Pinchiore, Florence's most famous restaurant. The restaurant has one of the World's great Italian wine lists. This wine which is made of 50% Sangiovese and 50% Merlot has a production of only 1500 bottles and can only be bought at the Enoteca Pinchiore.

Jyuri and Vittorio finally arrived after about 25 minutes. Vittorio who I knew from New York introduced me to his son Jyuri who I had never met before. Jyuri is the vineyard manager and assistant winemaker to his father.

Jyuri is very talented viticulturist, oenologist, and an all-around great guy. Roberto is Vittorio's other son who I got to know when he was my wine salesman from Winebow, the company that distributes the Fiore's wine in the United States. Since this trip I've gotten to know Jyuri pretty well as he comes to New York once in a while to promote Il Carbonaione. Roberto was not around, he was in Milano where he now lives and works.

Jyuri gave us a memorable tour of the winery. He took us through their various cellars and as we were walking through one of the smaller rooms we noticed some beautiful legs of Prosciutto and Salami hanging. We would have the good fortune to taste some of that fine hand-crafted Salumi a little later in our visit. Jyuri told us that he had wanted to make the salami and prosciutto so he asked Dante if he would show him how to cure the hind-quarters and make some nice salumi. He made the Prosciutto with the help and instruction of the affable Dante and I'll tell you that I have not tasted any better than theirs. They were scrumptious.

After showing us the fields and taking us through the cellars, Jyuri took us to thei tasting room which was a small building that was once the Village

School-House. The school Dante went to as a young boy so many years ago. The lure continues.

We then tasted the special wine that the Fiore's make for Enotecca Pinchiori as well as the Il Carbonaione 1995 and a barrel sample of the 1999 Vintage. Jyuri cut some of the fabulous Salami and Prosciuttto and my buddy Jimmy and I were in "7th Heaven" to be drinking the great wines of Podere Scalletta in their special tasting room with the owners while eating the wonderful Salumi that "The Great Dante" and Jyuri had crafted together by their very own hands. The food, the wine, the people, and setting were more than one could ever ask for. "It was Fabuloso!!!!"

On this trip to Tuscany we also went to the winery of Fattoria Quercia across from The Fattoria Valle.

It was a really nice little operation that is run by the lovely lady Laura whom we chatted with for a few minutes while sipping some of her tasty Chianti. On the entire trip of drinking great wines, Laura's was definitely one of our favorites, we shipped a case back to New York to enjoy at our dinner parties throughout the coming year.

We went to Badia Colto Buono in Gaiole which is owned by Lorenza de Medici of the most noble Florentine family of the Renaissance and patrons of Michael Angelo and Raphael.

We stopped off at Terrabianca in Radda to see our good friend Roberto Gundelar and his daughter Maya. They showed us around their beautiful winery that is run like a Swiss Clock as the Gundelers are from Zurich and partly of Italian ancestry on Roberto's mothers side of the family.

Roberto and Maya took us through a complete tasting of all their famous wines. First we tasted their excellent Chardonnay, a grape variety that I usually disdain from Tuscany, but their's is quite nice. The Terrabianca Chardonnay is outstanding of course or Roberto won't make anything less than very good to excellent and beyond. We also drank the fine Chianti "Croce", the perfectly balanced 100% barrique aged Sangiovese of "Cipresso," the great "Campaccio," "Cepate", and their fine example of Vin Santo to finish off the tasting and a most enjoyable time, another of many delightful visits and three more to go on The 2001 Italian Wine Tour.

We then made our way down to Montalcino to visit with Serina Columbini at the historical Fattoria Barbi, one of the oldest estates to be producing Brunello d' Montalcino.

We toured the great storied cellars that are filled with many exquisite Slovenian Oak Cask which are filled with wine made from mostly that precious Sangiovese Grosso for Barbi's celebrated Brunelloand Brunello Riserva, along with their Barbi

Brusco and Rosso d' Montalcino. The cellars of Barbi are really quite stunning, to see all those large cask of brilliantly kept oak, all lined in such an orderly fashion, a majestic sight that one rarely gets to see, "If Ever." Cellars such as Barbi's are something special to behold and when you are in one as stately as theirs you feel as if you have stepped back to a Magical Point in time. A time that no longer exists, and here you are, within it. It's a Grand place to be. After our visit to Fattoria Barbi we made a stop at Azienda Lisini, a small boutique type producer of some marvelous Brunello.

After Lisini it was off to see Paulo at Poggio Antico. Poggio Antico is one of Montalcino's top producers of outstanding Brunello, Rosso d' Montalcino, and bright fruity olive oil.

All-in-All our wine expedition of Tuscany was filled with awe-inspiring times at my friend's extraordin-arily beautiful Wine Estates in the most magnificent settings imaginable.

We had festive Lunches and Dinners, eating the World's best salami, succulent Bisecta al Fiorentino, Pasta's dressed with all sorts of sumptuous meat ragu's made with; Veal, Beef, Rabbit, and the native Wild Boar as we drank many of the local Super Tuscan wines, Brunello, and the storied Chianti right in the locale where they are made. Drinking these great wines with the fabulous local cuisine, our trip was a Gourmand's delight!

We lugged back to New York some World Class Wine and smuggled in some of the equally famous Salami from Forloni and Dario Cecchini (the famous "Singing Butcher") along with some Pecorino Toscano, Aceto Baslamico, Italian Anchovies, great Tuscan Olive Oil, and Pecorino Toscano, all items to add a little bit of Italy, from Italy to future dinner parties. Quite a memorable trip, and memories that will last a lifetime.

"The BUTCHER the BAKER"
The ITALIAN-AMERICAN PORK STORE

In earlier times up unto the Nineteenth Century, "The Butcher, "The Baker," and "The Candlestick Maker" were some of societies most respected and necessary citizens. They provided light, bread, poultry, meat, pastries, and cakes to the local citizenry. Even far into the Twentieth Century there were still many small villages in Italy and other parts of Europe where some families did not have an oven, so they would bring things such as Casseroles, pans of Lasagna, and Stews to the baker for him to cook their food in the bakery ovens.

Since the advent of electricity the candlestick maker is no longer a necessity to everyday life.

Because of convenience foods and supermarkets neither are the butcher and to some extent the baker. In this day and age the baker is still important for holidays and special occasions like birthdays and weddings. The butcher however is used by a very small percentage of the total population; most Am-erican's opting for the meat isle at the local Supermarket.

For those of us of Italian ancestry the butcher is of extreme importance, especially in the areas of fresh Pork Sausage, Braciole, and properly cut Veal Scallopines.

For Italian-Americans, there are usually two different types of butcher shops that we deal with. There is the very personalized tiny butcher shop that usually just sells fresh cut meat and poultry as well as fresh made sausages. In the once predominately Italian Neighborhood of Southern Greenwich Village down into the Northern part of Soho there are two fine butchers that have been used by the Italian's of the area for years. There is "Pino's" on Sullivan Street next to St. Anthony's and Florence Prime Meat Market on Jones Street between Bleecker and West Fourth Street. These shops are two good examples of the small neighborhood butcher shops that were prevalent in cities and towns all over the country, prior to the advent of the "Supermarket." These shops which are dwindling to small numbers are run by master meat cutters who will cut your steaks, chops, and cutlets to order, just the way you like it.

The other type of butcher shop that Italian-Americans frequent is known as a Pork Store. The Pork Stores have master butchers the same as the regular small shops, but in addition to purveying fresh meat, they sell many other food products.

Items that are staples of Italian Cooking. Many of the products imported from Italy, include; Pasta, Prosciutto di Parma, Olive Oil, vinegars, Porcini, Salami, Italian Cheese, Mozzarella, Cured Olives, Anchovies, Italian Tuna, and the like.

If you were ever pressed to pick one item sold at an Italian Pork Store or butcher shop that is most important to Italian-Americans, it would have to be without question, fresh Pork Sausages made on premise. To Italians, Sausage is like a religion. It is of great importance and a necessity of weekly living. There are not many self-respecting Italian-Americans who would ever even think of buying mass produced sausage at a supermarket.

The fresh Italian Pork Sausage is a necessity to make the Beloved Sausage and Pepper Sandwiches, to make Orechetti with Brocoli Rabe and Sausage, to add to a Sunday Sauce (Gravy), for making Pollo al Scarpariello (Shoemakers Chicken), and an assortment of other dishes. Yes, good fresh Italian Sweet and Hot Sausage is vital.

Every true Italian has their own favorite shop that makes the Sausage just the way they like it. Mine are both Florence Prime Meat Market on Jones Street in The Village or Faicco's. It's a toss-up, they are both great. I especially love the Sweet Sausage from Florence, it is perfectly seasoned with garlic, salt, and black pepper, and they also make the most

278

wonderful Lamb Sausages as well. The best and most famous Pork Store in the Village is Faiccco's Pork Store, which is right around the block from Florence.

If you want to make Braciola, whether it is of beef or pork, the butcher is of great importance. You need to have your meat cut and pounded in a specific way to make the Braciole. Also, if you're in a pinch for time to make the Braciole yourself, most good Italian butchers make very nice Braciole that are all tied up and ready for cooking in your own sauce. I usually get mine at Faicco's where they season them just right, with Beef or Pork of the highest quality.

Also of great significance to Italians is good quality Veal, especially when it comes to the subject of Scallopines and Cutlets for making dishes like; Veal Picatta, Saltimbocca, Veal and Peppers, Veal Parmigianino, and Veal Milanese. Now to the baker and I think we'll forget the candlestick-maker, although if you want to get the most beautiful hand dipped candles you'll ever see, I can tell you where to get them. There is a wonderful little shop in the tiny village of Sugarloaf, New York, about an hour's drive north of New York City where you can get the most beautiful Candles in the World. Truly amazing!

Back to the baker. In many of our Bellino family dinners over the years, my aunts would make delicious cakes and cookies sometimes but not always.

It is more than enough just to prepare all of the savory food of Antipasto, Pasta, and main course. When cooking a meal, you may not have time to make Sweets, but you want to serve Dessert. This is where the Baker comes in.

At any of our family meals, dessert and coffee is extremely important, for after we are finished eating the previous courses we usually sit around the table for another two to four hours drinking Espresso with Anisette along with some sweets of Italian Pastries and Cookies. We chat and tell stories, especially Uncle Frank. One or more guests would stop at the Italian Bakery and get all sorts of goodies to munch on with coffee. Things like; Cannoli, Sfogiatelle, Eclairs, and assorted Italian Cookies, so the baker was, and still is of extreme importance to us all year long, not just at the holidays and birthdays but practically every Sunday when we have the celebrated "Bellino Sunday Supper" at Aunt Fran and Uncle Tony's house in Lodi.

I know that many people all over the country get together and have the same type of big wonderful family meals as our family does. Sadly I know that there are some people who never do.

I hope this book will inspire people to get together with friends and family to share a beautiful meal and happy moments, whether you have never had the opportunity before, or if you have not done so for a while, may you be sparked to organize a festive dinner for the first time or to renew an old tradition.

ON ITALIAN FOOD

The pure essence of Italian Food, what is it? The long and short of it is; cooking the freshest, best quality ingredients in a manner in which the main ingredient shines and is not overpowered by any other element. The main ingredient should shine, whether it is veal, pork, lamb, fish, or a vegetable, the main ingredient should be the Star. It may be enhanced with different seasonings, but not over-powered by them. In-other-words, if you are roasting a whole fish like a Branzino or any other type of fish, one of the best ways to cook it in a true Italian manner would be to season it with just salt and pepper, roast it until it is just done or what the French would term "al point." Bring the roast fish to the table, filet it and sprinkle the filets with just a touch of olive oil and a squeeze of lemon. It's short, simple, sweet, and tasty. "That's Italian."

Keep it fresh, keep it simple and uncluttered. Want to grill or panroast a perfect steak? Go to your butcher and get some great Prime Steaks. Make sure you have a very hot grill or frying pan, brush a thin coat of oil on each steak, season liberally with salt and pepper and cook it for about four or five minutes on each side and your set.

Most Americans think Tomato Sauce is loaded with oregano and cooks for hours on the back burner of the stove. First of all, most tomato sauces made in Italy are made in less than thirty minutes and hardly ever contain oregano. The tomato being the main ingredient, the taste of the tomato should shine through and not be covered up by too many herbs or over cooking.

In making a true Italian tomato sauce the tomatoes are seasoned with garlic, olive oil, basil, crushed red pepper, and salt. "Basta!! That's it." Good spaghetti pomodoro is the utter essence of Italian cooking, so don't forget to get the best impeccably fresh ingredients and keep it simple.

"That's Italian!"

Here are a few recipes from various family members. All these dishes are great favorites of Italian Americans. The dishes are all very tasty and easy to make. Many take only twenty to thirty minutes from start to serving time.

Some of the dishes that I have included are known as foundation recipes, whereby once you know how to make the basic dish, you will be able to make many others dishes simply by using the same method but with different ingredients.

Try the recipes. They are easy. Experiment and build your own repertoire of the Italian and Italian–American Classics.

CAPONATA

Caponata, one of Sicily's classic dishes, third in popularity after Cannoli and Pasta con Sarde (Pasta with Sardines). Caponata is a tasty dish of sweet and sour eggplant stew, that's quite versatile.

It can be served on its own, on a sandwich, or with other items in a wonderful mixed antipasto. Caponata makes a great accompaniement to any grilled meat, chicken, and especially fish and it is great to stuff into sandwiches.

Caponata like many other famous dishes will vary in taste from cook to cook. I have eaten it numerous times in Italy and New York and after trying many different versions, I've come up with my own famous recipe that is based on the one that my friend Gino makes. Gino C., who is originally from Siracusa in Sicily, learned how to make Caponata from his father who was the original chef of their restaurant and is now retired.

Because of the content of salt, sugar, and vinegar, Caponata keeps well for up to two weeks and makes a great gift to any Italian food lover when it is present-ed in a nice mason jar. You can change this recipe to suit your own taste if you'd like, but it should always contain the eggplant and it should be sweet and sour (agro dolce).

CAPONATA RECIPE

2 large eggplants, washed and cut into
¾" cubes, do not remove skin from Eggplant
½ cup olive oil
3 medium onions, cut into ¼" dice
1 small Red Pepper and 1 Yellow Pepper
Cut into ½" dice
2 Ccelery stalks, ¼" dice
¼ raisons, soaked in hot water for 15 minutes
1 ½ cups Tomato Sauce
6 tablespoons sugar
6 tablespoons Baslamic vinegar
2 teaspoons salt, 3 teaspoons black pepper
3 tablespoons of capers

1) Saute the peppers in a large pot with ½
   of the olive oil for 10 minutes

2) Add the onions and sauté over low heat
   for 15 minutes.

3) Add the celery and tomato sauce and
   continue simmering. While the other
   ingredients are simmering, Brown the
   eggplant in several batches in a large frying
   pan with remaining olive oil. Add the browned
   eggplant, sugar, and vinegar to the pot and
   simmer. Cool and serve.

BRUSCHETTA

Ingredients:
8 ½" slices of good crusty Italian bread
8 ripe fresh plum tomatoes cut into ½" cubes
16 fresh basil leaves, chopped
2 peeled garlic cloves
½ lb. fresh mozzarella, 1/" dice
Salt & pepper

1)
Grill bread on each side over a charcoal grill if
you can or under the broiler of an indoor oven.
2)
Rub the toasted bread with garlic cloves.
Brush the bread with extra virgin olive oil.
3)
Mix tomatoes with basil, olive oil, salt,
and pepper.
4)
Spoon the seasoned tomatoes onto the bread.
You have the option of making the bruschetta
with just tomatoes, or add Mozzarella as well.

NOTE: You can make Bruschetta with many different
toppings like: escarole or Broccoli Rabe sautéed in
olive oil and garlic or with Zucchini or Eggplant. The
choices are many, use traditional ones, experiment,
and have Fun!

CROSTINO PARADISO

I invented this tasty appetizer that's great to pass around with other hores'dervres to guest while they drink an Apertivo before dinner at a Cocktail Parties. These crostini are quick and easy to prepare and the name matches the feeling you get when you eat them, you feel as if you're in "Paradiso."

10 oz. button mushrooms, sliced and sautéed
¼ lb. Fontina Cheese, ¼ lb. Prosciutto
Truffle Oil, 2 Tbs. chopped fresh parsley
1 baguette (French Bread) cut in ¼" slices
and lightly toasted

1) Saute Mushrooms and season with Salt
   and Black Pepper

2) Cut Fontina & Prosciutto into pieces
   That will cover the bread.

3) Place a few mushroom slices and a piece
   of Prosciutto on each slice of bread and
   sprinkle with truffle oil.

Cover with Fontina. Put the crostini ina 400 degree Oven for 4 minutes. Sprinke crostini with chopped Parsley and pass around to guests.

LUCIA'S STUFFED PEPPERS

This was one of my Mothers best dishes.
We always ate it as a main course but it's
also excellent as an appetizer on its own
or as part of a Hot Antipasto.

Ingredients:

1 medium onion, minced
3 cloves of garlic, minced
6 Tbs chopped parsley
6 Tbs. bread crumbs
2 eggs.   Salt & pepper
1 cup long grain rice
¾ lb. ground pork
¾ lb. ground beef
1 Tablespoon Dry Oregano
½ cup grated Pecorino Romano
4 Red or Green bell peppers
½ cup chicken broth
1-1/2 cups tomato sauce

Preparation for Lucia's Stuffed Peppers:

1) Cook the rice for 12 minutes in boiling
water and drain.

2) Cut the tops off the peppers and reserve.

3) Mix all remaining ingredients except the
Broth and sauce in a Large bowl.

4) Stuff the peppers with the meat mixture
And top with the Pepper tops.

5) Place the peppers in a small baking pan
with the the broth. Cover with aluminum
foil. Bake at 350 for 40 minutes. Remove
foil and continue Baking for 15 minutes longer.

6) Heat the tomato sauce.

7) Put 6 Tbs. of sauce on a plate with a pepper.

8) Serve with grated cheese.

FRITTATA

Frittata, a flat Italian Omlette that can be made with an endless variety of ingredients from spaghetti and tomato sauce, spinach and ricotta, with mushrooms, zucchini, sausage & peppers, potato with onions, or a thousand other fillings.

Frittata are great to eat anytime of the day. They are flat and round and can be cut into wedges like a pie. This makes for the perfect treat to pack in a lunchbox or to take on a picnic to eat with some bread, salami, fruit, and cheese. Make traditional Italian Frittata and experiment with whatever ingredients you like best to make your very own specialty.

SPINACH and RICOTTA FRITTATA

1 lb. fresh spinach, washed and roughly chopped
½ cup Parmesan Cheese, 1 cup ricotta, 10 extra
large eggs
¼ stick butter, salt & pepper to taste

1) Break eggs into a bowl. Add salt & pepper
   and beat eggs well.

2) Put the spinach and butter into a 9" nonstick
   pan and sauté over medium heat for 5 minutes.
   Season with Salt and Pepper.

3) Raise heat to high. Add eggs and sauté until
   The eggs are half cooked. Add ricotta and
   Parmigiano and continue sautéing for 1 min.

4) Place in 350 degree oven for about 8 minutes.
   Remove, and cut Frittata into 10 wedges
   and serve.

NOTE: *Once you have mastered the basic tech-*
nique, you will be able to make many different kinds of
frittata simply by changing the ingredients. You can
use whatever combination of meat, fish, vegetables,
poultry, and or cheese that you desire and can
imagine. Experiment, invent, have fun.

SAUTEED GREENS

If you don't already know, green vegetables
are without a doubt the single best thing along with
water, that a person could ever put in their body.
Quite healthy. Italians love all sorts of fruits and
vegetables and serve them in a multitude of ways.

Any green vegetables that are simply sautéed in
garlic and olive oil are great favorites. Along with
being immensely beneficial to good health, looking
good, and tasting great, these sautéed greens are
quick and easy to prepare.

Sautéed greens are the perfect accompaniment
to any meat, fish, or poultry entrée and are great
on their own or with other ingredientsin an antipasto
or as bruschetta on grilled or toasted Italian bread.
You can prepare Brocoli Rabe, Escarole, Swiss Chard,
Green Beans, Broccoli, Spinach, or Beet Greens all
in this manner.

SAUTÉED ESCAROLE

Ingredients:

2 heads escarole washed and roughly chopped
7 cloves garlic, peeled and sliced
¼ teaspoon cruched red pepper, ¼ cup olive oil

1) Blanch escarole in boiling salted water for
   2 minutes. Drain off water. Drain again
   And squeeze excess water from Escarole.

2) Saute garlic in oil until it just begins to brown.

3) Add red pepper and escarole. Saute escarole
   over Medium Heat for about 6 minutes.
   Season with Salt and black pepper and serve.

LENTIL SOUP

This soup is a marvel! It's cheap and easy to make, it's nutritious and tasty and you can eat it for breakfast, lunch, dinner or anytime at all. Make a large batch and eat some right away, put some in the frig for later in the week, and freeze some to eat a couple weeks down the road. You can make several different soups from this basic recipe by adding pasta, Escarole, or sausage. Eat it with a salad as a starter and some good bread and you have a complete tasty meal.

LENTIL SOUP Recipe:

10 oz. dry lentils, 4 Tbs. olive oil
3 medium onions, diced. 3 cloves garlic, chopped
3 stalks celery, chopped. 3 carrots, diced large
1-1/2 cups plum tomato's chopped
½ cup diced Ham, Bacon, or Pancetta
6 cups chicken broth, salt, and pepper to taste

Lentil Soup Preparation:

1) Saute the bacon or pancetta and drain
   the oil off.

2) Add onions and garlic and saute over
   a low flame for three minutes.
   Add carrots and cook 8 minutes longer.

3) Add tomato's, chicken broth and lentils.

4) Bring to boil. Lower heat and simmer until
   The Lentils are tender. Tender yet a little
   firm, about 45 minutes.

5) Serve in soup bowls as is or you can
   add a little short pasta to each bowl.
   Drizzle extra virgin olive oil on top and
   pass around the Grated Parmigiano.

ZUPPA MARIATA (Italian Wedding Soup)

This is a wonderful Neapolitan soup that is served at weddings in and around Napoli and by Italian-Americans in all over the U.S.. A small bowl can be served as a starter and this soup is more than hardy enough to be served on its own as a complete meal. Children especially love it because of the little meatballs, "Children of all ages that is."

Ingredients for Italian Wedding Soup:

¾ lb. ground beef and ¾ lb. ground pork
1 cup grated Parmigiano, 1 clove garlic, minced
¼ fresh parsley, finely chopped. 1 bay leaf
1–3 lb. broiler chicken, 6 whole cloves garlic, peeled
8 cups water, 4 cups chicken broth
1 large onion, chopped. 2 carrots diced
1 head escarole, finely chopped

PREPARATION:

1) Combine ground meat, eggs, parsley, minced garlic, and Parmigiano. Season with salt & pepper. Shape into Meatballs, about the size of a large Marble.

297

2) Place whole chicken, whole garlic, bay leaf, and water in a large pot and bring to the boil. Lower heat and simmer for 1 hour and 15 minutes.

3) Place meatballs in a lightly oil baking pan and cook in a 350 Degree oven for 8 minutes.

4) Remove chicken from pot and set aside to cool. Add Carrots and onions and broth and continue cooking.

5) Remove chicken meat from bones and dice. Add diced Chicken back into the pot with Meatballs simmer for 15 Minutes. Add escarole and cook 10 minutes.

6) Add a little cooked pasta to each soup bowl. Ladle soup into bowls, making sure each person gets 5-6 Meatballs. Pass around the grated Parmigiano and Enjoy!

PASTA e FAGOLI

*Pasta e Fagoli, Pasta & Bean Soup, the "Big Boys"
say, "Pasta Fazoo.". However you say it, Pasta
Fagoli is a unabashed Italian and Italian-American
favorite. Here's my secret recipe that was taught to
me by a great cook from Brindisi named Pasquale.*

2 medium onions, 3 celery stalks, 2 carrots, minced
½ lb pancetta, minced finely.   ¼ cup olive oil
8 cloves garlic, peeled an cut into thirds
1 lb. dried cannelini beans,
soaked in water overnight
2 sprigs fresh rosemary. 1 bay leaf
1 ½ cups canned plum tomatoes
4 cups chicken broth
4 cups water. Salt & pepper to taste
1 lb. ditalini

Preparation:

1)   Sauté pancetta in a large pot for 3 minutes.
     Add garlic & onions. Sauté for 6   minutes
     on low heat.

2) Add celery and carrots. Sauté for 4 minutes.

3) Add tomato's, beans, broth, & water. Bring
   Up to the boil, then lower to a slow simmer
   And cook for 1 ½ hours until the beans are
   tender.

4) Remove half the beans and mash through a
   foodmill or puree in a blender.

5) Place the mashed beans back into the pot
   with the whole beans.

6) Put remainder of olive oil in a pan with 6 cloves
   of garlic, a bay leaf, and rosemary. Cook over
   medium heat for 6 minutes. This is called a
   perfume.

7) Strain the perfume into the pot of soup, mix
   and simmer the soup with perfume for 12
   minutes.

8) Cook the ditalini according to instructions on.

9) To serve, put ½ cup cooked ditalini in a soup
   bowl. Fill the bowl with the bean soup.
   Sprinkle a little Extra-virgin olive oil over
   the soup. Pass around Parmigiano and enjoy.

ON COOKING PASTA

Let's get a few things straight right off the bat. You do not put oil in the water that you cook the pasta in. This is an American wives tale. Secondly, you do not drain pasta and run cold water over it unless you are using it for a cold pasta salad or you are cooking pasta sheets for lasagna.

NOTE: You should read the directions on the pasta package and you should start testing the pasta for doneness 2–3 minutes before the suggested cooking time.

The Pasta should be cooked almost all the way through while remaining slightly firm in the middle. This is al dente (firm to the bite).

Fresh pasta cooks faster than dried pasta and is usually cooked through in about three minutes.

Fresh pasta can never be cooked al dente as it Is not dried and hard in the middle. Only dry pasta can be cooked al dente.

TOMATO SAUCE

The great thing about tomato sauce besides its taste and simplicity is that once you know how to make it then you have the base to make more than 100 other sauces simply by adding different ingredients to this basic sauce. You can make Mushroom Sauce for pasta, simply by slicing and sautéing Mushrooms, add them to your Tomato Sauce, cook two minutes, and you're set, you now have Mushroom Sauce ready to toss with your Pasta of choice. Spaghetti, Farfalle, or Rigatoni would all be good choices. You can do the same with Eggplant, Zucchini and peppers or whatever ingredients you choose.

Contrary to what many people think you do not simmer tomato sauce for hours and hours on the back of the stove as you do with a Sunday Sauce or some type of Meat Ragu. When making a tomato sauce you can cook it for as little as fifteen minutes and no more than an hour and fifteen minutes. Basta!!

So here's the recipe. Go to it.

TOMATO SAUCE RECIPE

Ingredients:
2-28 oz. cans San Marzano crushed tomatoes
or other good quality Italian style tomatoes
4 cloves minced garlic
1 small onion, minced
½ teaspoon crushed red pepper
¼ cup virgin olive oil
¼ chopped fresh basil or 1 teaspoon dried
Salt and pepper to taste

1) In a 6 quart or larger pot, sauté onions over
   a low flame for 3 minutes. Add garlic and cook
   for 3-4 mins. Do not let the garlic get dark
   or burn.

2) Add tomatoes, turn heat up to high and stir.
   When sauce starts to bubble, turn flame
   Down so the sauce is at a low simmer.
   Simmer for 45 minutes while frequently
   Stirring the bottom of the pan to keep
   sauce from burning. Add fresh basil in
   the last ten minutes of cooking.

3) Cook whatever pasta you choose (spaghetti
   is best) according to directions on package.
   Drain pasta, toss with tomato sauce and a
   drizzle of olive oil, plate, and serve w/Cheese.

MEATBALLS!!!!!

Spaghetti and Meatballs! What's more Italian than that? A lot of things actually. There is a constant ongoing debate over whether "Spaghetti and Meatballs" is an authentic Italian dish or not.

Of course spaghetti is very Italian and so are Meatballs, however Italians do not eat them together, this is an Italian–American tradition and a great one at that, as Lidia Bastianich and other have written. Italian–American is a great cuisine in itself. It is most truly authentic Italian with a few twist here and there, like eating Meatballs on the same plate with Spaghetti instead of two separate courses as they do in Italy. What's wrong with that? Maybe the Italian–American mammas of way back (turn of of The Century, around 1900) didn't want to clean twice as many dishes so they combined the two courses into one. Maybe they didn't own two dishes per person. Just kidding.

Let me tell you one thing, in case you didn't know. Meatballs are infinitely more popular in the United States than they are in the mother country of Italy. Americans eat millions more of them a year than their Italian brethren. The Neapolitans and Sicilians eat them the most in Italy and because of the fact that these are the areas where the greatest number of Italian immigrants to the U.S. came from, thus one of the reasons this dish became such a great favorite of Italian expatriates, their children, grandchildren, and millions of Americans, including people of other ethnic origins who happen to love Italian and Italian-American food. It is one of the world's great cuisines. You don't have to be Italian to love their food, the same as many Italian-Americans love to eat Chinese food. It's tasty, so Mangia!!!

MEATBALL RECIPE:

Ingredients:

1 lb. ground Beef
½ lb. ground Veal
½ Pound Ground Pork
4 Tbs. fresh Italian Parsley, chopped
1 minced onion
2 cloves garlic, minced
4 Tablespoons plain breadcrumbs
2 large eggs
Salt & pepper
½ cup grated Parniggiano or Pecorino

Note: If you want, instead of this beef, pork, and veal proportions, you can use just Beef (2 lbs.) or 1 lb. Ground Beef & 1 lb. Veal.

PREPARATION:

1) In a small bowl, break and beat eggs. Add breadcrumbs and let soak for 10 minutes.

2) In a large bowl, add all the remaining ingredients. Add eggs and mix well with your hands.

3) Shape meat mixture to from balls that
Are about 2 inches in diameter.

4) Coat the bottom of a cookie sheet or
roasting pan with a thin film of olive oil.
Cook Meatballs at 350 degrees for 10 minutes.

5) Take meatballs out of oven and simmer for
one hour in a batch of tomato sauce from
the previous recipe.

6) Serve Meatballs with Spaghetti for the
Classic Italian American favorite
Spaghetti and Meatballs or do as the Italians
do, especially the Neapolitans and serve the
sauce first with Spaghetti, Rigatoni, or ziti.
Serve the Meatballs as the main course with
a Salad or potatoes on the side.

SUNDAY SAUCE

Sunday Sauceis the famed pasta sauce, also known as "Gravy"of which a multitude of Italian-Americans have been cooking for some hundred years now. It is the favored dish for the ritualistic Italian Sunday meal, when the whole family gets together for their favorite foods. Every family has their own special way of making "Gravy" (Sauce), from the type of pasta it is served with, whether it's Rigatoni, Ziti, Gnocchi, or Cavatelli. It is this sauce that brings the family together, at least once a week.

Sauce or "Gravy"as you might call it depending where you are from, is also known as "Ragu", or "Sunday Gravy." The meats that can be used in any combination that the cook likes best are; Meatballs, Sweet or Hot Sausage, Lamb, Beef, or Pork Neck, Spareribs, Braciole, and Chicken Legs or Thighs. Experiment and develope your own special family recipe.

My own favorite combination of meats are, Meatballs, Sweet Sausage, and Pork Ribs. Sometimes I might add Chicken thighs or substitute beef or pork neck for the ribs, it depends on my mood, what I feel like eating most, and what is or is not available. I always make the "Sauce" with Meatballs because one of biggest reasons for making a "Sunday Sauce" along with having an amazing Sunday Dinner, is to have Meatballs to make Meatball Parm Sandwiches with on Monday, for what we like to call Meatball Parm Mondays. "Yeah baby" !!!

The Sunday Sauce is practically a religious experence. Enjoy it, making it, eating it, talking about it, sharing it!

There are no statistics on it, but this sauce has done more to keep families together, unifying and strengthening them along with nourishing the participants while giving them a reservoir of fond memories to nurture their minds, bodies, and souls.

SUNDAY SAUCE (a.k.a. GRAVY)

Ingredients:

½ cup olive oil
2 medium onions, minced
12 cloves garlic, minced
7-28oz. cans of crushed tomatoes
2 lbs. spareribs
2 lbs. sweet Italian sausage
2 cups chicken broth
1 Teaspoon crushed red pepper
1 ½ teaspoons salt
1 tablespoon black pepper
1 batch of Meatballs from
previous Meatball recipe

Preparation:

1) Place onions in olive oil in a large pot
   (at least 12 quarts).
   Sauté on a low flame for four minutes.

2) Add all the tomato's and chicken broth.
   Raise flame to high. Bring the tomatoes
   up to the boil, then lower the sauce to a
   very low simmer

3) Cut the spareribs in-between the bones so you have individual Ribs. Add to pot.

4) Place sausages in a separate pot fill with water. Bring to boil, then simmer for 10 minutes. Drain the sausages and add to pot with sauce.

5) Make the previous recipe of meatballs up to the point where they have cooked in the oven for 10 t minutes.

6) Let all ingredients simmer for 1 hour and 15 minutes.

7) Add meatballs to pot and let simmer one hour longer.

8) Serve the sauce with your favorite Short Pasta such asRigatoni, Gnocchi, or Ziti.

NOTE: *The sauce should simmer on a very low flame. It is important to stir the bottom of the pot with a wooden spoon every few minutes to keep the sauce from burning.*

SPAGHETTI with BROCCOLI

This is a dish similar to a Southern Italian favorite Broccoli Rabe and Pasta. This dish is made with regular Broccoli rather than the bitter Rapini (Broccoli Rabe). It is fast and easy to make. On top of that it's really tasty and quite healthy.

2 heads fresh broccoli. 6 colves thinly sliced garlic
¼ cup olive oil, ¼ teaspoon crushed red pepper
1 ½ lbs. good quality imported Italian spaghetti
¼ cup grated Parmigianno Regianno
1/3 stick of butter

Preparation:

1)   Wash broccoli and cut into florets. Blanch
     Broccoli in boiling salted for 3 minutes.

2)   Drain broccoli in a strainer. Place olive oil
     and garlic in a large frying pan. Saute over
     low heat until the garlic just start browning.
     Add broccoli and sauté over medium
     heat for about 6 minutes.

3)   While the broccoli is sautéing, cook spaghetti
     in a large pot of water according to directions
     on the Pasta package.

4)   Drain spaghetti and add to pan with Broccoli.
     Add butter and toss. Plate Spaghetti with
     Broccoli and pass around the Grated Cheese.

NOTE: A variation on this dish is to add 1 cup of
cooked Tomato Sauce to the spaghetti after draining
it from the water. Plate the Spaghetti into six plates
or pasta bowls, divide the sautéed broccoli evenly on
top of each portion of Spaghetti, grate on Parmigianno
and serve.

ORECHIETTE con SALSICE e RAPINI
"Orechiette with Sausage and Brocoli Rabe"

Ingredients:

1 lb.Imported Italian Orechiette
4 links Hot or Sweet Italian Sausge
1 lb. fresh Brocoli Rabe washed and cut into
1 ½" pieces
¼ cup Olive Oil
¼ teaspoon Hot Red Pepper flakes
1/3 cup grated Pecorino, salt and Black Pepper
4 cloves Garlic peeld and coarsely chopped
1/8 teaspoon Crushed red Pepper Flakes

Preparation:

1) Fill a large pot with 6–7 qts. Water and bring
   to boil. Add 3 table spoons salt to water, then
   add Brocoli Rabe, cover pot and boil for three
   minutes.

2) Remove the broccoli Rabe with a slotted
   spoon from water and keep on the side.

3) Place 3 tablespoons olive oil in a large
   skillet. Add the Sausage and cook over
   medium heat until the sausage is completely

314

cooked through. As the sausage is cooking, break the sausage with a wooden spoon into pieces that are about a inch–and–a–half around.

4) Cook Orichiette in a large part of boiling that are about a inch–and–a–half around.

5) After the sausage has been cooked through, remove sausage from pan with a slotted spoon and set aside. Add the garlic to pan and a little more olive oil, if needed. Add Peperoncino. Saute the garlic over medium heat for about two minutes, then add the Broccoli Rabe and sauté for about five minutes over low to medium to heat. Season with Salt & Black Pepper to taste.

6) Drain cooked Orichiette from water, reserving 3 tablespoons of water to toss with pasta. Add drained oriciette and water to pan with Broccoli Rabe. Add sasauge, toss and cook over medium heat for two minutes.

7) Serve 4–6 equal portions on plates or in pasta bowls. Sprinkle olive oil and grated Pecorino over Orichiette. Serve and enjoy!

SCHIAVELLI PASTA

This is my version of Vincent Schiavelli's Pasta cu Vraccula Arriminatu (pasta with cauliflower) that my friend Ada loves so much. Vincent includes anchovies and saffron, which Ada does not like so I have altered the recipe to suit her taste. I love Vincent's recipe with the anchovies and saffron but this is just another version and it should illustrate to people that recipes in cookbooks do not have to be followed to the letter and you can change them around, because you may not have all the ingredients available or simply to comply with your own taste. So remember you can always experiment with recipes. Have fun, and explore.

SCHIAVELLI PASTA

1 large head cauliflower, core and cut into
1-1/2" pieces
10 cloves of garlic, peeled
2-28 oz. cans crushed San Marzano Tomato's
1 medium onion, minced
½ teaspoon crushed red pepper
¼ cup olive oil, salt and pepper to taste

1) Place half the oil in a large pot with the minced onions. Sauté for three minutes. Add five cloves of garlic that have been thinly sliced. Sauté for 3 mins. over low heat. Add Red Pepper, sauté for 2 minutes.

2) Add tomatoes and simmer over low heat for 45 minutes.

3) While tomato sauce is simmering, place remainder of olive oil in a large frying pan and sauté the cauliflower over medium heat for 12–15 minutes until it is slightly browned.

4) Add remaining 5 whole garlic cloves with cauliflower. Sauté for about 5 minutes. Add salt & pepper to taste.

5) Add cauliflower to tomato sauce and Cook for 10 minutes.

6) You can use almost and pasta for this sauce, although short pasta such as Rigatoni, Ditalini, orichetti, or Cavatappi work best.

7) Cook the pasta according to directions on package, drain, pour sauce over pasta and mix.

8) Serve with grated Pecorino Romano
   or Parmigianno Reggiano.

NOTE: If you'd like to use anchovies and saffon
like Vincent does, you can add a pinch of saffron
and three minced anchovy filets at step number
(4), saute' for two minutes. Continue to # 5 .

BUCATINI all' AMATRICIANA

This tasty sauce made with bacon originates from Abruzzo but is most famous in Rome where it is found on menus all over the city. The meat used in the sauce in Italy is Giuancialle or Pancetta (un-smoked bacon). In my recipe I use pancetta and smoked bacon. I once had two Gentlemen from Abruzzo at my former restaurant Bar Cichetti order the Rigatoni Amatriciana that I had made for a special one night. They were flabbergasted that it was so good. They really couldn't believe an American could make their native dish taste so delicious.

I couldn't believe it when they showed up the very next night to eat the Amatriciana again. After the meal they told me that they couldn't believe how good it was, and that they came back to eat it again because it was the best Amatraciana they had ever eaten; better than any in Abruzzo or Roma where the dish is a local specialty. "I kid you not."

This was a major compliment coming from Italians who when it comes to food "Do Not Lie." So this was compliment coming from two men from Abruzzo was one of the greatest I've ever received in my professional culinary career. Truly.

AMATRICIANA SAUCE alla BELLINO

3 medium onions, liced thinly. ¼ cup olive oil
1 teaspoon crushed red pepper, 1 Tbs. minced
fresh Rosemary
1 lb. smoked bacon and ½ lb. pancetta diced
2–28 oz. cans crushed tomatoes
3 cloves garlic, minced
kosher or sea salt and black pepper to taste
1 & 1/2 lbs. imported Italian Bucatini or
other pasta

1) Place bacon and pancetta in a large frying
    pan and cook over very low heat to render
    fat (about 12 minutes).
    Do not brown or let bacon get hard or crispy.

2) Remove bacon and pancetta from pan and
    set aside. Drain all but 3 tablespoons of fat
    from pan. Add olive oil and onions to pan
    and sauté over low heat for about 12
    minutes. Add garlic and red pepper,
    sauté for three minutes.

3) Add tomato's, bacon, and pancetta.
   Simmer for 30 minutes.

4) Add rosemary. Simmer for 15 minutes.

5) Cook Bucatini or other pasta. Drain pasta,
   sprinkle with olive oil. Add sauce, mix
   and plate. Serve with grated Parmigiano.

RAGU BOLOGNESE

2 tablespoons olive oil
1 medium onion, minced
2 celery stalks & I carrot minced
2 lbs. ground beef and 1 lb. ground veal
3 cups red wine, 1 cup chicken broth
2-28 ounce cans crushed San Marzano Tomatoes
1 oz. dried Porcini Mushrooms, soak in hot water
10 minutes to soften Mushrooms
5 tablespoons of sweet butter

Preparation:

1) Put olive oil, celery, onion, and minced
    carrot in a large pot. Sauté over a low
    flame for 5 minutes. Add ground meats to
    pot and cook until the meat has lost its
    raw color. Do not brown the meat or it
    will get hard. Break the meat up with
    a wooden spoon as you ar cooking it.

2) Drain the fat off the meat mixture in
    a strainer. Put the drained meat back in
    the pot and season with Salt and Pepper.

3) Add wine and cook over high heat
    Until the wine is reduced by half.
    Add tomatoes, Porcini and broth.

4) Cook the sauce over the lowest flame
    possible for 2 ½ hours while stirring every
    few minutes to keep the sauce from burning.

5) When sauce is finished cooking, turn off
    flame and stir butter into sauce.

6) Cook the pasta of your choice, Tagiatelle
    is most traditional for Bolognese Sauce, but
    you may use Spaghetti, Rigatoni, or Fusilli.

7) Drain the cooked past and mix it with some
    of the sauce and a knob of butter. Serve with
    grated Parmigiano.

RIGATONI al FORNO

This is a great dish for parties and large groups
of people.It is delicious and it can be made hours ahead
of time or the day before a party and reheated in the
oven.

Ingredients:

1 lb. mozzarella cut into ½ inch cubes
1 cup ricotta
2 lbs. rigatoni, 1 ½ grated Parmigianno
1 ½ lbs. sweet sausage simmerd in water
for 12 minutes
Meatballs from Meatball recipe rolled into
1" diameter each
8 cups tomato sauce from previous recipe

1) Prepare Tomato Sauce and Meatballs from
    Previous recipes. Roll the meatballs into
    1" Meatballs. Roast the Meatballs in 350
    degree oven for 15 minutes.

2) Cook the rigatoni for a few minutes less
    than package states (about 7 minutes)
    as it will cook further in oven.

324

3) In a large baking pan that will be big enough to hold the ingredients, line the bottom of pan with tomato sauce.

4) Mix the cooked pasta with 5 cups of sauce, Mozzarella and slice Sausage.

5) Place half the mixture into pan. Put a light coat of sauce over the mixture. Dot with ½ the meatballs and Ricotta and sprinkle with some Parmigianno. Repeat this procedure until the pan is full.

6) Bake for 50 minutes at 350 degrees.

7) Plate and serve with grated Pecorino or Parmigianno.

FETTUCCINE ALFREDO

In the 60's and 1970's Fettuccine Alfredo was one of the great favorite dishes on Italian restaurant menus throughout the country. It was in the late 80's that the popularity of the dish started to wane for a couple of reasons, one being the Genesis of the health movement in The United States and two being the start towards more authentic Italian dishes and the almost total disdain of the so-called cliché dishes, Fettuccine Alfredo being one of them.

Being in the restaurant business, I have people request this dish to me several times a week. Let me tell you, "this is the sign of a great dish, regardless of what anyone thinks otherwise." Fettuccine is quick any very easy to make, once you know how to make the sauce, you will be able to make a number of other dishes simply by changing or adding different ingredients.

You can make Tortellini Panna by substituting tortellini for the fettuccine, add a few cooked vegetables like mushrooms, peas, carrots, and broccoli florets and you have another hugely famous dish of the 70's and 80's, "Pasta Primavera", supposedly invented at Le Cirque and still, though not on the menu a very popular dish there. You need to be "In-The-Know" to order it.

When I was a Sous Chef at the hugely popular Caio Bella Restaurant, one of the hot trendy restaurants of the late 80's, I used to make a dish called "Fettuccine Lemone" that only the regulars knew about.

It was not on the menu. If you were in-the-know and knew of it, you could get it. I used to make this dish for a rich Oil Baron's daughter from Kuwait and you can make it too simply by adding the zest from a couple lemons to the basic Fettuccine Alfredo recipe, and a few leaves of Fresh Basil is nice too. Bon Apetito!

RECIPE for FETTUCINE ALFREDO

Ingredients:

1 lb. fresh Fettucine
1 pt. heavy cream, ½ stick butter
1 cup grated Parnigianno
2 egg yolks, salt & pepper

1) Put the cream in a large frying pan. Bring
   to the boil, lower the flame and let the
   cream cook. Season the cream with salt
   and pepper to taste. Reduce volume by
   One-Third, This will thicken the sauce.

2) Cook the fettucine and drain it. Put the
   fettucine in to the pan with the cream.
   Add butter and stir.

3) Turn the flame off. Add egg yolks and
   Parnigianno and stir. Serve and pass
   around extra Parmigiano.

Note: You can make *Fettucine Lemone* by adding
the zest of two lemons to this recipe. Fresh basil
is also another nice addition for the Lemone Sauce.

CHICKEN CACTITORE

Ingredients:

3 Tablespoons olive oil
1 large Onion, sliced thick
6 chicken thighs and 6 legs
2 red bell peppers, thinly sliced
8 garlic cloves, peeled
8 oz. button mushrooms cut into quarters
2 cups whole canned San Marzano tomatoes
salt and pepper to taste, ¾ cup dry white wine

Preparation:

1) Salt and pepper pieces of chicken to taste.
   Put olive in a large frying pan and brown
   Chicken on all sides.

2) Remove chicken from pan and set aside.

3) Put peppers and garlic into pan. Saute
   over high heat for 5 minutes. Add
   mushroom and onions, season with
   salt and pepper, cook for 8 minutes.

4) Remove vegetables from pan. Put chicken back in pan with wine. Cook over medium heat until wine is reduced by half.
Add tomato's and cook for 8 minutes.

5) Put the rest of the vegetables back into the pan. Cover and cook at a low simmer for 35 minutes.

6) Serve as is with a salad or vegetable.

CHICKEN SCARPARIELLO
"SHOEMAKERS CHICKEN"

Chicken Scarpariello, "ShoeMakers Chicken."
That's what my Grandfather Philipo was, a shoe-
maker from Lercara Freddi, Sicily. The same town
that Frank Sinatra's grandfather was also a Shoe-
maker in. My Mother's Father Philipo Bellino and
Mother (Josephina) immigrated to the United Staes
through the Port of New York through Ellis Island
in 1904. My Grandfather Philipo Bellino opened a
shoemaker-shop on Main Street in Lodi, New
Jersey (Soprano Territory). This dish is not that
well known by most Americans apart from those
of Italian Ancestry, of which it is a great favorite.

Ingredients:

1 whole broiler chicken cut up into 8 pieces
4-6 links of fresh Italian pork sausage,
either sweet or hot, or a combination
2 sprigs of rosemary
2 red bell peppers cut into ¾ inch slices
8 garlic cloves
crushed Red Pepper and Salt & Black Pepper
to taste

Preparation:

1) Blanche sausage in simmering water
   for 8 minutes.

2) Season chicken with salt and pepper.
   Place chicken in a large frying pan
   With olive oil and brown chicken on
   all sides. Remove chicken from pan
   to a platter. Cut sausage into four
   pieces each and brown in frying pan.
   Add peppers and cook over medium
   heat for 7 minutes.

3) Add chicken back into pan. Cover pan
   and cook over a low flame for 15 minutes.
   Take cover off pan, add rosemary and
   continue cooking for 8 minutes.

4) Serve two pieces of chicken with sausages
   and peppers to each person. Serve with
   a salad or roast potatoes.

CHICKEN and/or VEAL PARMIGIANNO

Ingredients:

4 boneless Chicken Breast pounded to half
their original thickness or 4 Veal Cutlets from
your butcher if you are making Veal Parmigianno
½ cup all purpose flour
2 eggs beatened and seasoned with salt & pepper
1 ½ cups plain bread crumbs, ½ lb. mozzarella
1 ½ cups tomato sauce, ½ cup grated Parmigianno
1 cup vegetable or peanut oil for frying

1)   Season cutlets with salt & pepper. Place flour,
     eggs, and bread crumbs in 3 separate shallow
     bowls.

2)   Heat oil to 375 dgrees in a large frying pan.

3)   Bread cutlets first by dredging them in flour.
     Shake off excess flour. Dip cutlets into eggs
     and let excess egg drip off. Thirdly place
     cutlets in bread crumbs and completely
     cover by pressing crumbs into them.

4)   Fry cutlets until they are golden brown
     on both sides.

5) Get a shallow baking pan that is just large enough to hold all the fried cutlets. Coat the bottom of the pan with half the tomato sauce. Place the cutlets in the pan over the tomato sauce. Coat top of cutlets with the remainder of the sauce.

6) Sprinkle grated Parmigianno over cutlets. Top the cutlets with thin slices of Mozzarella. Bake for about twelve minutes in a 375 degree oven.

7) Serve with your favorite green vegetable, a tossed salad, or whatever you like.

NOTE: The method of making Chicken Parmigianno or Veal Parmigianno is the same, the only difference is whether you use veal cutlets or chicken breast.

Also note that making this dish with Pork is another delicious and economical alternative to using Veal.

THE NEGRONI

Basic Recipe:

1 ½ ounce Campari
1 ½ ounce Sweet Vermouth
1 ½ ounce Gin
Ice
Orange

1) Fill a Rocks–Glass or Highball Glass with Ice.
2) Add Campari, Sweet Vermouth, and Gin.
3) Stir ingredients. Garnish with a piece of Orange Peel or slice of Orange.

THE BELLINO NEGRONI

For me, this is the Perfect Negroni. The basic Negroni recipe calls for 3 equal parts (1 oz. or 1 ½ oz.) each of Cmapari, Sweet Vermouth, and Gin in a glassfilled with ice, and garnished with an Orange Peel.

For the most Perfectly balanced Negroni, I put in slightly less Campari (1 ¼ oz.), 1 ounce of Gin, a little more Sweet Vermouth with 1 ½ ounces, over Ice, shake, add a Spalsh of Club Soda and Garnish with a good size piece of Orange Peel or Orange slice. Voila! The Perfect Negroni. Enjoy!

FINAL THOUGHTS

Dear Reader,

I do hope you enjoyed reading this book, the stories and experiences in it. The main theme of the book and its stories are about people gathering around the table, friends, family, or people you just met. The table doesn't necessarily have to be a table, it is a metaphor for just gathering anywhere for food. It can be at the counter of a Hot Dog stand, in a car, in the woods, or sitting on a Park Bench with sandwiches on your laps. Some many of us have done a multitude of times, with a nice Sub, with a beloved Meatball-Parm, a tasty Sausage and Peppper Hero.

However, the table we most talk about in the book, is when you gather with family or invite friends over for a nice home-cooked meal. There is something quite special about these kinds of meals, in which friends are invited into one's home.

Do not think that just because you are having a dinner party that it needs to be extravagant or fancy. Something as simple as Spaghetti with Tomato Sauce and a tossed green salad accompanied by a nice loaf of bread and maybe a modest little wine, is perfectly fine. It can be Hamburgers or just sandwiches. The thing is to get together with people you like, gather round the table to "Break Bread" so to speak, with friends and or family, eating together, chatting, laughing, maybe even crying. You share and gather memories and good times. Memories that lastLifetime.

"Do it! Enjoy!"

Daniel

La TAVOLA QUICK GUIDE

Dear Reader,

I wrote and have inserted the La Tavola Quick Guide as just that, I Quick Guide that will help and any reader who might want and be in need of a quick suggestion and some more information on some of the best Italian Restaurants, Caffe's, Pastry Shop, Bread Bakers, Pork Stores, Pizzerias, Italian Specialty Food Stores of all kinds, food, wine, and dining establishments that might be helpful to you in whatever way you might need. I've listed various dishes as the Best of ; Best Pizza, best Cannoli, Best Espresso, etc..

Yes these are my picks and I know others might disagree on whose Pizza, Meatball Parm, Bolognese Suace or what-not is or isn't best. I've been eating great Italian Food all my life, have traveled extensively throughout Italy and along with working in the business for almost 30 years have studie the subjects inside and out for just as long. So?

I hope this guide is helpful to you. This book La Tavola is actually in a way a guide-book on a whole but not in guide-book form. In the many stories in the book which are written as stories, there is quite a lot of information on a number of subjects that pertain to the theme of this book, which is "spending time at the table (Tavola) with friends and Loved-Ones eating and drinking Italian Food and Wine," chatting and what not, having a good time at the table. Within these stories such as Sunday Sauce, The Feast of The 7 Fish, New york's Real Little Italy and others, there is a multitude of information on Italian and Italian-American Food in restuarants, Caffe's, Pork Stores, Bakeries, specialty shops, in Italy, in Greenwich Village, on Arthur Avenue, whereever. Quite a lot of information. You need to read the stories to get the info, and I hope you do or you all ready have. There's quite a lot of interesting things. The guide is just to be able to go back and be able to get some quick info after you're finished reading the book. A way to quickly find out and remember that great Pork Store, where to go to get some of the best Pizza in town (Best Pizza in the World), who has the tastiest Cannoli, or New York's best Bolgnese.

Please keep in mind that this little guide in back of the book is just that, a little guide, and although very helpful and a good amount of great info, recommendations, and suggestions, the amount of info in this guide in the back is just a small fraction of all the great goodies of information and stories that proceeded the guide. If you read the whole book or a good portion of it, you all ready know this fact.

And as concerns how to read the book, you can of course read it cover to cover, starting at the beginning and ending here, which is best. You can, as I sometimes do with certain non-fiction books, pick out one or two chapters of special interest, read them, then go to the beginning of the book and go from the beginning and on to the end. Regardless of how you go about reading the book, again I thank you and hope you have or will enjoy reading it.

Thanks,
Daniel

Favorite Italian Restaurants NY

1) Bar Pitti ..6th Ave., Greenwich Village
2) Villa Mosconi ..Macdougal Street, NY NY
3) Elio's .. 2nd Avenue near 84th St., NY NY
4) Patsy's (56th Street .. Sinatra's Favorite)
5) Rao's "If you can get in!" Probably not!
6) Ballato .. East Houston Street, NY NY
7) Frankie's Spuntino (Brooklyn)

Favorite Pizzeria's

1) Totonno's ..Neptune Ave. Coney Island
2) DiFarra's .. Avenue J, Brooklyn, New York
3) John's Pizzeria .Bleecker St. Greenwich Village
4) Lombardi's .. Spring Street
5) Bella Blu .. Lexington Ave., NY NY
   Only Great Pizza on Manhattan's "UPS"
   Upper East Side, until you hit Patsy's in
   East Harlem.

Favorite Italian Pastry Shops

1) Rocco's ..Bleecker St., Greenwich Village
2) Bella Ferrara ..Mulberry Street, Little Italy
3) Viniero's .. East 11th Street, East Village

Favorite Pork Stores

1) Faicco's ..Bleecker St, Greenwich Village

Favorite Butcher Shop

1) Florence Meat Market .. Jones St., W. Village
2) Pino's Meat Market, Sullivan Street, Soho

Best Italian Cheese Shops

1) DiPalo's ...Grand Street, little Italy
2) Russo's ...East 11th Street, East Village
3) Joe's Dairy, Sullivan Street, Soho

Best Italian Caffe

1) Caffe Dante ...Macdougal St.,Gr. Village
2) Caffe Reggio ..Macdougal St., Gr. Village

Best Old School Italian–American Décor

1) John's Restorante .East 12th Street, E. Village
2) Caffe Reggio ..Macdougal St. Gr. Village

Best Cannoli in The City

1) Rocco's Pasticceria ..Bleecker Street

Best Bolognese Sauce

1) Villa Mosconi ..Macdougal St.,Gr. Village
2) DeGrezia Restorante, East 50th St., NY, NY
3) Monte's .. Macdougal Street
4) My House . Somewhere in Greenwich Village

Best Espresso

1) Caffe Dante, Macdougal St., Greenwich Village
2) Sant Ambroeus .. West 4th St., Gr. Village

Best Espresso Beans for Home Brew

1) Porto Rico Coffee Co., Greenwich Village

Best Negroni in New York

1) Pat Parotta's House ..Staten Island, NY
2) Sant Ambroeus ..West 4th Street, Gr. Village

Best Linguine/Spaghetti Vongole

1) Ballato, ..East Houston Street, Noho, NY NY

Best Coda d'Vacinara (Oxtails)

1) Bar Pitti .. 6th Avenue, Greenwich Village

Best Lasagna

1) Elio's .. Second Ave. near 84th Street, NY NY
2) Monte's .. Macdougal Street, Greenwich Village

Best Spaghetti and Meatballs

1) Patsy's .. West 56th Street, Theater District

Best Veal Milanese

1) Da Silvano .. Sixth Avenue, West Village

Best Meatball Parm

1) Defonte's Sandwich Shop ..Gramercy Park
2) Frankie's Spuntino .. Brooklyn
3) Spunto ..Carmine Street, Greenwich Village

Best Sausage and Peppers Sandwich

1) Lucy's .. at San Generao and all Italian Festivals in New York

Best Angolotti

1) Barbetta .. West 46th Street, Theater Dist.

Best Italian Sausages Sweet & Hot

1) Faicco's .. Bleecker St., Greenwich Village

Best Lobster Tail ...
"The Pastry Not the Crustasean"

1) Bella Ferrara .. Mulberry St., Little Italy

Best Italian Bread

1) Parisi Bakery .. Elizabeth Street, Noho
2) Sullivan Street Bakery, New York, NY

Best Baked Clams Areganata

1) Ballato, East Hosuton Street, Noho, NY NY
2) John's .. East 12th Street, East Village

Best Speedino alla Romana

1) John's .. East 12th Street, East Village

> *The Speedino alla Romano at John's*
> *Restorante in The East Village is*
> *absolutely "Amzaing" They make it*
> *to perfection, in all its gooey fried*
> *melted Mozzarella glory! Yumm!*
> *Not only does John's make thee Best*
> *Speedino I've ever tasted, they may*
> *very well be making Manhattan's only*
> *one of this formely standard Old-School*
> *Red Sauce Italian-American restaurant*
> *specialty. I'm sure there are places in*
> *Brooklyn still making this great old*
> *Red-Sauce-Restaurant "standard."*
> *Thank you John's for still making this*
> *beauty, "please don't ever stop," and*
> *thank you also for preserving the won-*
> *derful old décor of John's and not ruin-*
> *ing it as the owners of "Lanza's"*
> *around the block did.*
> *John's is a "Museum Piece" and a part*
> *of New York and America's Italian-*
> *American history and heritage.*
> *Thanks!*

Best Italian Wine List

1) Barbetta .. West 46th Street, Restaurant Row

   Barbetta's Wine List is "Insane" meaning
   unbelievably Great .. No place in town comes
   close .. Babbo and Del Posto get all the Press,
   but as the Big Boys say, "Fugggettabout It" !!!!
   They can't touch Barbetta, which has more
   Verticals of Great Barolo Crus than any place
   in the World, including Peimonte. They've got
   an extensive number of Barbaresco and Brunello
   verticals as well, along with great Chanpagne,
   Amarone, Taurasi, and-on-and-on.
   Like I Said, "The Wine List is Insane."
   Insanely Good !!!

Best Bolito Misto

1) Del Posto ..10th Avenue at 16th, Meatpacking

The Bolito Misto at Del Posto is as they say
"Off the Chain," Great! I Friggin Love It. You
can not get any better anywhere in New York, if
you can find it. Not many places in town make,
almost none as a matter–of–fact. Even in Italy
you'll not get many better than Chef Mark
Ladner's, which is as good as it gets. If you've
never had it, "Try it sometime," you'll not
regret. I garauntee.

Best Prosciutto

1) DiPalo's .. Grand Street, Litlle Italy

Best Sopressetta

1) Faicco's .. Bleecker St., Greenwich Village

Best Broccoli di Rabe

1) Da Silvano .. 6th Avenue, Greenwich Village
2) DeGrezia .. East 50st Street, NY NY

Best Ravioli and Fresh Pasta

1) Pastosa Ravioli .. Brooklyn, New York
2) Piemonte Ravioli .. Grand Street, NY NY
3) Raffetto's Fresh Pasta, 144 Houston St.

100 Year Old Italians

1) John's .. East 12 th Street .. Since 1908
2) Raffetto's Pasta .. Houston Street
3) Barbetta .. West 46th Street .. Since 1906
4) Caffe Reggio ...Not 100 Years Old, but ???
5) Raffetto Pasta Co.,144 Houston Street, 1906
6) Porto Rico Importing Company .. Since 1907
   Porto Rico Coffee Importing Co.
   Bleecker Street, New York, NY
   "Yes it's Italian" Owned and operated by the Longo Family in Greenwich Village since 1907

A Note from the Author

This book was written in 2006 and published a few years later. Some of the people in the book are sadly no longer with us, but I have left the stories as they were originally written by me at the time (2006).

Some of the places like Vesuvio's and Zito's have closed, Sadly, but I have left the different stories as I wrote them originally.

I have changed the book a little, adding things as I saw fit and had a few different ideas, so there are a few small pieces where a story may appear as it is in the present day when the book was first published in 2012. Do not forget that the bulk of the book (90%) was written in the year 2006, Never-the-Less, the stories remain the same.

I hope you have enjoyed.

Daniel

For photos and more on "La Tavola" Italian American Food, updates, and the Italian- American Experience, go to:

http://sunday-sauce.blogspot.com/

Comments and corresondance welcome.

Made in the USA
Lexington, KY
07 May 2016